QUIZ PRIX

The motorsport quiz prix where your knowledge of motor racing decides whether you can become a world champion.

For 1 or more players

By

Neil Simmons

ALL TRACK CIRCUIT IMAGES IN THIS BOOK ARE SUPPLIED BY

© RacingCircits.info

PUBLISHED BY

CHEQUERED PRESS

Author: Neil Simmons
Twitter: @SimmoWriter

Editor: Steph Barraclough
Twitter: @Stephloves4

Publisher: Chequered Press
Twitter: @CheqPress

Circuit Images: RacingCircuits.info
Twitter: @RaceCircuitInfo

Supporting Partner: RaceStaff.com
Twitter: @Race_Staff

ISBN: 978-1-070-60335-3

ABOUT THE AUTHOR

Neil is a former press officer in sport and police officer. He started writing freelance for motorsport in 2001 for various publications. His passion for motor racing was born in 1976 and that battle between James Hunt and Niki Lauda. From there he developed a love for the 24 Hours of Le Mans. He is a big Fleetwood Mac fan and a lifelong McLaren supporter. Neil is married, owned by a cat and can normally be found drinking copious amounts of tea. He writes post-apocalyptic fiction under the pen-name of Simon Neilson.

OTHER WORKS BY THE AUTHOR

Under the pen-name of Simon Neilson

NOVELS

Rogue Evacuation*
The Circus
The Apocalypse Room
Children Of The World's End
Chronicles Of The Apocalypse

AUDIO DRAMAS

Children Of The World's End
Chronicles Of The Apocalypse
The Survivor Journals

published by Wild Wolf Publishing

"For my best friend Duggan.

My golf coach, motor racing partner in crime and rallycross hospitality gate crasher.

The best friend I could ask for."

CONTENTS

QUIZ PRIX CIRCUIT - QUESTIONS

QUIZ PRIX CIRCUIT - ANSWERS

FOREWORDS

'In the absence of an A-Level in Motorsport, Quiz Prix should be on the National Curriculum. [It should also come with a free anorak and bobble hat] Highly addictive and infuriating, this incredibly fact-rich book proved to me that Plato was right when he wrote: "All I know is that I know nothing" Oh, that's Greek philosopher Plato, not Jason Plato (two-time BTCC Champion, 2001 & 2010)'
Neil Cole - Motorsport Presenter & Commentator
Twitter: @neilcole

'Welcome to Quiz Prix! Here in this quiz book you will be asked questions over thirty two rounds. Take on your friends, family or even play as a sole player. This is your chance to show off your motorsport knowledge as you collect championship points for every correct question you get. This book will get your mind racing and head scratching as you race to get the answers, you do not want to get any wrong or you may find yourself at the bottom of the championship standings. You will find various questions where you will have to remember famous drivers, teams, cars or even a name of a circuit and much more. Will you cross the finish line in first place or find yourself scrambling for points trying to overtake your rivals? Before the lights go green, read the instructions carefully before you hit the throttle pedal. Welcome to Quiz Prix. Good Luck'
Chris Wheeler – British Rally Driver
Twitter: @CWheelerRally

'Appreciating the twists and turns of the courses which races take place on is one of the key aspects of racing for many motorsport fans. So, knowing Adelaide from Ahvenisto, Kyalami from Knutstorp and Zolder from Zandvoort is all part of the fun. We are delighted to be able to provide the track maps for Quiz Prix and hope it inspires you to find out more about circuits around the world through our site'
Neil Tipton - Founder of RacingCircuits.info
Twitter: @RaceCircuitInfo

INTRODUCTION

The thing I have always loved most about motorsport is that unlike football, cricket, rugby or tennis, no two seasons of the sport are the same. No two circuits are identical to each other, even in the oval racing world.

Formula One cars change completely from one season to the next, and every driver has their own style, personality and even technique.

It's the only playing field where men and women can compete evenly, and in an environment where money talks and reputations are everything, the sport never fails to capture my very soul.

Nerds like myself will find this book to be more than just a trivia quiz challenge on the theme of motorsport. It is a celebration of the sport's history, its legacy and its diversity, and encompasses everything about the sport I hold dear.

The format is fabulously addictive and a great way to indulge your passion for racing. I will waste hours of my life on planes, trains and probably automobiles too addicted to this book.

An absolute must have for petrol-heads everywhere.

Jake Sanson – Motorsport Commentator
Twitter: @JakeSanson

RULES

The rules to the quiz are pretty simple but it depends whether you are going to attempt the quiz yourself or have a championship with a group of friends.

At the front of the book is the contents table. At the end of the book will be the answers to the circuit questions, the page numbers will also be listed in the contents page.

There will be 20 questions per circuit, except for the final round at the Circuit de la Sarthe, where at this iconic track you will compete in the "24 QUESTIONS OF LE MANS".

It is time to decide whether you play on your own or with a group of friends.

ONE PLAYER

If you decide to play on your own, then you can go through each circuit and try to score as many championship points as you can, to test your motor racing knowledge.

MULTI-PLAYER

The fun way is to get a group of like-minded racing friends or family together and have your own championship.

There are 32 circuits, or 32 rounds. You and your friends attend each circuit to answer the questions.

A question master can be designated, or you can take it in turns to ask questions each round and just write down your answers. Once a round is finished, total up the number of correct answers and you can allocate championship points from the table on the following page:

NUMBER OF CORRECT ANSWERS AT CIRCUITS	CHAMPIONSHIP POINTS TO ALLOCATE
0	0 points
1	1 points
2	2 points
3	3 points
4	4 points
5	5 points
6	6 points
7	7 points
8	8 points
9	9 points
10	10 points
11	11 points
12	12 points
13	14 points
14	16 points
15	18 points
16	20 points
17	22 points
18	24 points
19	26 points
20	30 points
21*	35 points
22 *	40 points
23 *	45 points
24*	50 points

places 21st to 24th are for the final round at the Circuit de la Sarthe and the 24 Questions of Le Mans.

After the 30 rounds are complete, place all players in order of how many championship points they have achieved and the player with the most points is crowned the Quiz Prix champion.

At the rear of the book you will find boxes to keep record of your championship standings.

The maximum championship points any player can achieve over the 32 circuits equals 980 points.

How close to that target can you get?

Grab some scrap paper and pen or pencil for your answers and its lights out and away we go!

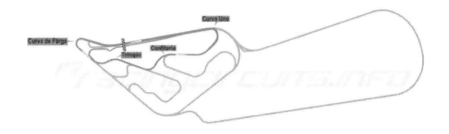

ROUND 1

AUTODROMO

JUAN Y OSCAR GALVEZ

1. The first World Championship Formula One race was held at this circuit in 1953. Which Italian driver won the race?

2. Which American motorcycle racer, riding a Suzuki, won the last 500c Argentine Grand Prix held at the circuit in 1999?

3. The 1000km Buenos Aires race, part of the old World Sportscar Championship, used most of this circuit. In 1956 Argentine driver Carlos Menditeguy won, but which British driver did he share the car with?

4. Michael Schumacher won the Argentine Grand Prix in 1998. Which team was he driving for?

5. The last World Sportscar Championship race to be held at the circuit was in 1972. Ronnie Peterson and Tim Schenken won the race, but which make of car were they driving?

6. At the 1998 Argentine motorcycle Grand Prix, which Italian won the 250cc race?

7. Which Formula One driver won back-to-back Grand Prix's in 1995 and 1996?

8. Which Formula One constructor has the most Grand Prix wins at the circuit, a total of four?

9. Which Australian rider won the 500c motorcycle Grand Prix in 1994?

10. Which South African Formula One driver won the 1977 Argentine Grand Prix at this circuit?

11. Who was the last Brazilian driver to win a Grand Prix at this circuit?

12. Which former American Formula One world champion won the 1000km of Buenos Aires on two occasions, both times in a Ferrari?

13. Which American rider won the 500c motorcycle Grand Prix in 1987?

14. Who is the only Canadian Formula One driver to win the Argentine Grand Prix at this circuit?

15. From 1972 until 1981 the same engine manufacturer won the Argentine Grand Prix at this circuit. What was the manufacturer?

16. Jo Siffert and Derek Bell won the 1000km of Buenos Aires in 1971. Which make of car were they driving?

17. Who was the only French Formula One driver to win the Argentine Grand Prix at this circuit?

18. Mercedes won their first and only Argentine Grand Prix at this circuit in 1955. Who was the winning driver?

19. Which Italian rider won the 125cc Argentine motorcycle Grand Prix in 1999?

20. Which driver won the 1980 Argentine Grand Prix at this circuit and went on to win the World Championship that season?

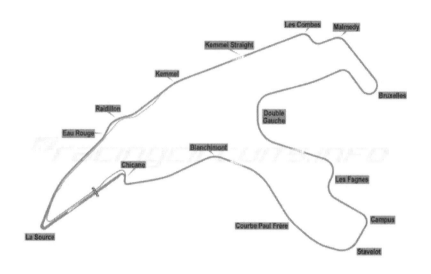

ROUND 2

CIRCUIT DE

SPA-FRANCORCHAMPS

1. Which World Rallycross and DTM champion was part of the team who won the Spa 24 Hours in 2011, driving an Audi R8 LMS?

2. Prior to 2019, in what year did Williams last win a Formula One Grand Prix at Spa?

3. Which former British Formula One driver won the 6 Hours of Spa in 2004 driving an Audi R8 with co-driver Jamie Davies?

4. Which Formula One driver won the Belgian Grand Prix at this circuit from 1988 to 1991?

5. What is the name of the tight first corner at Spa-Francorchamps?

6. Which British racing driver teamed up with Sebastien Buemi and Nicolas Lapierre to win the 6 Hours of Spa in 2014 for Toyota?

7. Laurens Vanthoor, Rene Rast and Markus Winkelhock won the 24 Hours of Spa in 2014. What car manufacturer supplied the team they were driving for?

8. Who won the first Formula One World Championship Grand Prix at Spa in 1950?

9. Nigel Mansell won only one Belgian Grand Prix at Spa, in 1986. Which Formula One team was he driving for that day?

10. Prior to 2019, who was the last Italian Formula One driver to win a Formula One race at Spa?

11. Kimi Raikkonen won four Grand Prix's at Spa from 2004 to 2009. Which team was he driving for when he won his first Grand Prix at the circuit?

12. Which manufacturer won the 6 Hours of Spa five years consecutively from 2007 to 2011?

13. From 2015 until 2018, which car manufacturer won three Spa 24 Hour races?

14. Which Formula One constructor won the Belgian Grand Prix at Spa for four years in a row from 1962 to 1965?

15. What is the name of the corner at Spa which is often and mistakenly called Eau Rouge?

16. Which McLaren driver won the 2012 Formula One Grand Prix at Spa?

17. Between 1962 and 1966, the Belgian Grand Prix at Spa was won by a British driver. Jim Clark won four of them, who was the other British driver who won in 1966?

18. The 6 Hours of Spa has been part of endurance racing since 1953, but in which year was it introduced as part of the FIA World Endurance racing calendar?

19. Which former Ferrari and McLaren driver was part of the team who won the 1985 24 Hours of Spa driving a BMW 635 CSi as part of the European Touring Car Championship?

20. Two British drivers finished on the podium for the 1995 Formula One Belgian Grand Prix. Damon Hill finished second driving a Williams-Renault, who was the British driver in third driving a Ligier-Mugen-Honda?

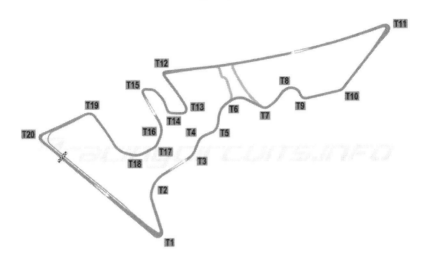

ROUND 3

CIRCUIT

OF THE

AMERICAS

1. Which former motorcycle 500cc World Champion helped to conceive the layout of the Circuit of the Americas?

2. Formula One raced at the Circuit of the Americas for the first time in 2012. Which driver won that race?

3. Which rider won the first MotoGP Grand Prix at the circuit in 2013?

4. Which British racing driver was part of the three driver team for Audi who won the 6 Hours Circuit of the Americas in 2013?

5. Kimi Raikkonen won the 2018 United States Grand Prix, but which driver was on pole position for the race?

6. World Rallycross was held at Circuit of the Americas in 2018. Which driver won the event?

7. In 2014 Scott Pruett and Memo Rojas won the Lone Star Le Mans race at Circuit of the Americas. Which team were they driving for?

8. Australian V8 Supercars visited Circuit of the Americas for the first and only time in 2013. The Austin 400 was a series of 4 races. Fabian Coulthard won one race for Brad Jones Racing, but which driver won the other three races for the Triple Eight Race Engineering team?

9. Which Lotus-Renault driver finished second in the 2013 Formula One United States Grand Prix at the circuit?

10. Which Italian rider finished third riding a Ducati at the 2016 Motorcycle Grand Prix of the Americas?

11. Up until 2019, across MotoGP, Moto2 and Moto3, only two British riders have won at the Circuit of the Americas. Sam Lowes is one, what is the name of the other British rider?

12. Mark Webber and Brendon Hartley were part of a three-driver team who won the 6 Hours of Circuit of the Americas in 2015 and 2016. Who was the third driver?

13. At the 2015 Formula One United States Grand Prix, Lewis Hamilton and Nico Rosberg finished first and second for Mercedes. Which driver finished third?

14. Which Spanish rider had won the Moto3 race in 2013 and the Moto2 race in 2016 at the Circuit of the Americas?

15. Jon Fogarty and Alex Gurney won the 2013 Grand-Am of The Americas as part of the Rolex Sports Car Series. What make of car were they driving for the GAINSCO/Bob Stallings Racing team?

16. At the 2017 6 Hours of Circuit of the Americas, the top 12 positions were taken by prototype cars. What was the make of the highest placed GT class car in thirteenth?

17. At the 2016 Motorcycle Grand Prix of The Americas Jorge Lorenzo finished second, but what make of bike was he riding?

18. From 2012 to 2018 only three Formula One Ferrari drivers have finished on the podium at the Circuit of the Americas. Sebastian Vettel and Kimi Raikkonen are two, who is the third?

19. When Formula One visited Circuit of the Americas for the first time in 2012 which team was Daniel Ricciardo racing for?

20. When MotoGP visited Circuit of the Americas for the first time in 2013 what make of bike was the former World Champion Nicky Hayden riding?

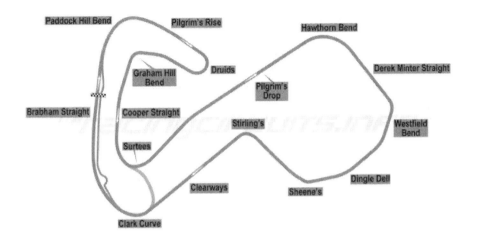

ROUND 4

BRANDS HATCH

1. The 2011 British Superbike Championship was decided in the last race of the final round of the season at Brands Hatch. Tommy Hill beat which rider by six thousandths of a second to take the title?

2. What is the name of the straight on the start/finish line directly after Clark Curve?

3. Which driver won the last Formula One Grand Prix held at Brands Hatch in 1986?

4. Which British driver won the British Grand Prix at Brands Hatch in 1964?

5. Yvan Muller, in the first round of the 2001 British Touring Car season, took pole position, set a fastest lap and won the race. Which car manufacturer was he driving for?

6. In the 2017 British Superbike Championship, three riders went into the last race at Brands Hatch to decide the title. Shane Byrne and Leon Haslam were two riders fighting for the title, who was the third?

7. The World Touring Car Championship featured at Brands Hatch from 2006 to 2010. Winning two races during that period, who is the only British driver to stand on top of the podium as a World Touring Car race winner at Brands Hatch?

8. The DTM series appeared at Brands Hatch between 2006 and 2013. Which British driver for Mercedes won on two occasions?

9. From 1993 until 2008 the World Superbike Championship featured at Brands Hatch. Who was the last British rider to win a series race there, completing a double race win in 2007?

10. The now defunct A1 Grand Prix of Nations raced at Brands Hatch from 2005 until 2009. Which Formula One driver won the main race for Germany in 2007?

11. Which future Formula One World Champion won three British Formula Three races at Brands Hatch in 1989 and twice in 1990?

12. The original Race of Champions was last held at Brands Hatch in 1983. Which Formula One driver won that race?

13. Who won the 1978 British Grand Prix driving for Ferrari?

14. The Formula One Grand Prix of Europe was held at Brands Hatch in 1983. Which driver, in a Brabham-BMW, won the race?

15. In the 2017 British Touring Championship at the last round held at Brands Hatch, three different drivers won the last three races. Aiden Moffat and Colin Turkington won the first two, who won the last driving a Toyota Avensis?

16. Which British rider won both World Superbike races at Brands Hatch in 1995?

17. Which French rider won the opening race of the 2009 British Superbike season at Brands Hatch riding a Suzuki GSX-R1000?

18. Of the six British Touring Car races held at Brands Hatch during the 2009 season, Matt Neal and Rob Collard won one each. Which driver won the other four races?

19. Driving a Lotus-Cosworth 72, which driver won the 1970 Formula One British Grand Prix?

20. What is the name of the hairpin at the bottom of Hailwoods Hill?

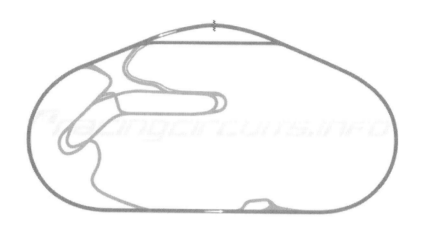

ROUND 5

DAYTONA

INTERNATIONAL

SPEEDWAY

1. Up to the 2019 season, which NASCAR driver had the most wins at the Daytona 500 with seven?

2. Which car manufacturer has the most wins at the Daytona 500?

3. In which American state is the Daytona International Speedway located?

4. Which Spanish driver teamed up with Jordan Taylor, Renger van der Zande and Kamui Kobayashi to take victory in the 2019 24 Hours at Daytona?

5. Until 2019, who was the last British driver to be in the winning car for the 24 Hours at Daytona?

6. The Daytona 200 is the motorcycle race held at the circuit. Which bike manufacturer had the most wins with 22 as of 2019?

7. Which 2006 MotoGP champion won the Daytona 200 in 2002?

8. Which driver won the Daytona 500 in 2017?

9. Which driver won the NASCAR Xfinity Series Coca-Cola Firecracker 250 race three times and went on to win the Daytona 500 twice?

10. Which car manufacturer has the most 24 Hours at Daytona wins?

11. Which British racing driver in 1986 won the 24 Hours at Daytona driving a Porsche 962?

12. Which car manufacturer won the 1992 24 Hours at Daytona with all its drivers coming from the same nation as the car manufacturer?

13. Which British rider won the 2008 Daytona 200 riding a Kawasaki?

14. In what year did a BSA bike last win the Daytona 200?

15. In what year was the first Daytona 500 night race?

16. Up to 2019, how many times has Joe Gibbs Racing won the Daytona 500?

17. Up to 2019, who is the only foreign-born driver to win the NASCAR Daytona 500?

18. Joey Legano won the 2015 Daytona 500, but which make of car was he driving for Team Penske?

19. Which former Williams and McLaren Formula One driver won the 24 Hours of Daytona in 2007 and 2008, driving a Riley MkXI-Lexus?

20. Which car manufacturer won the 24 Hours at Daytona with drivers Raul Boesel, Martin Brundle, John Nielsen and Jan Lammers?

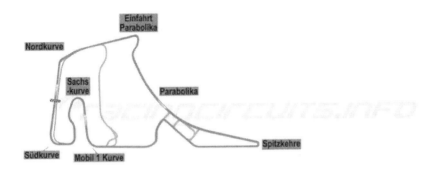

ROUND 6

HOCKENHEIMRING

1. In what year did the Hockenheimring host the Formula One German Grand Prix for the first time?

2. Which driver won the 1970 German Grand Prix at the circuit, driving a Lotus-Ford?

3. In World Rallycross, which driver at the World RX of Hockenheim won back-to-back events in 2016 and 2017?

4. Gary Paffett won round one of the DTM championship in 2010, but which other British driver won the round nine return at Hockenheim?

5. Which Formula One driver won the 2012 German Grand Prix at the Hockenheim ring?

6. Which driver won three German Grand Prix's at the Hockenheimring from 1988 to 1990?

7. What is the name of the first turn at the Hockenheimring?

8. Which rallycross driver won the first RX of Hockenheim in 2015?

9. Which future British Formula One driver gained pole position at the 2014 GP2 Series race held at the Hockenheimring?

10. Which British motorcycle rider won the 500cc Grand Prix at Hockenheim in 1973?

11. The last motorcycle German Grand Prix was held at Hockenheim in 1994. Which rider won the 500cc race on a Honda?

12. Which racing driver lost his life in 1968 at the circuit during a Formula 2 race?

13. Which Ferrari driver won the 1977 German Grand Prix at Hockenheim?

14. Nico Rosberg won the 2014 German Grand Prix at Hockenheim, but which Williams driver finished second on the podium?

15. Michael Schumacher won the 2006 German Grand Prix for a Ferrari first and second. Which driver was in the second placed Ferrari?

16. As of 2019, who was the last McLaren driver to win a Formula One race at Hockenheim?

17. Which German driver won the both races at Round 10 of the DTM championship in 2018?

18. At the 2013 round ten of the DTM championship, Timo Glock won the race, but what make of car was he driving?

19. Ferrari won the German Grand Prix at Hockenheim in 1999 and 2000. Rubens Barrichello won in 2000, but which Ferrari driver won in 1999?

20. Which Williams driver won the German Grand Prix in 2001?

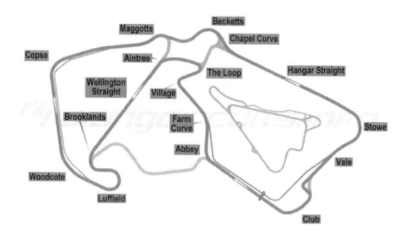

ROUND 7

SILVERSTONE

1. What is the name of the corner directly after the Hangar Straight?

2. Which driver won the first ever FIA Formula One World Championship Grand Prix at Silverstone in 1950?

3. MotoGP returned to Silverstone for the British Grand Prix in 2010. Which Spanish rider won the race?

4. World Rallycross moved from Lydden Hill to Silverstone in 2018. Which driver won the event?

5. Under the timed 6 Hour distance race at Silverstone, known in WEC as the 6 Hours of Silverstone, which German driver teamed up with Benoit Treluyer and Marcel Fassler in an Audi to win the race?

6. In Round 9 of the 2013 British Touring Car Championship, Jason Plato won the first two races at the circuit, which driver won the third?

7. For the three British Superbike races at Silverstone in 2017 three different riders won the three races. Glenn Irwin, Josh Brookes and Dan Linfoot were the winners, but what make of bike was Josh Brookes riding?

8. Who won the 1987 Formula One British Grand Prix at Silverstone?

9. Which British Formula One driver won back-to-back British Grand Prix's at Silverstone in 1999 and 2000?

10. Up to 2019, who was the last Australian rider to win a MotoGP British Grand Prix at Silverstone?

11. Which British rider won both World Superbike races at Silverstone in 2010?

12. Driving a McLaren-Ford, which driver won the 1975 Formula One British Grand Prix at Silverstone?

13. Up until 2019, the last time Red Bull won a Formula One race at Silverstone was 2012. Which driver won the race?

14. Which MotoGP rider won the 2015 British Grand Prix at Silverstone?

15. In the 2018 6 Hours of Silverstone, both hybrid Toyota's were disqualified due to excessive wear on their Skid Planks. Which non-hybrid LMP1 team took the race win?

16. Which British touring car driver, who went on to race in World Touring Cars, won the two opening British Touring Car races in Round 7 at Silverstone in 2010?

17. What is the name of the corner before the sequence of Maggots and Becketts?

18. Damon Hill won the 1994 British Grand Prix at Silverstone, but which Frenchman, driving a Ferrari, finished second?

19. Who was the last American rider to win a 500cc British Grand Prix at Silverstone?

20. Between 1991 and 1994, Williams won all the British Grand Prix's at Silverstone. Nigel Mansell won two and Damon Hill won one. Who was the other Williams driver to win during the period?

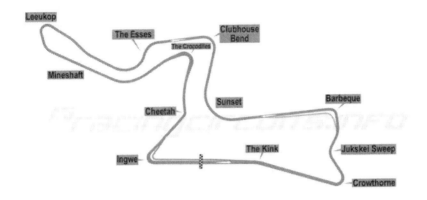

ROUND 8

KYALAMI

RACING CIRCUIT

1. In which year did Kyalami first host a Formula One world championship race?

2. The South African Formula One Grand Prix was last held at Kyalami in 1993. Which driver won the race?

3. Prior to 2019, the last time World Superbikes was held at Kyalami was in 2009. Which Japanese rider won both races?

4. Who was the first British Formula One driver to win a Grand Prix at Kyalami?

5. Jody Scheckter won his home Grand Prix at Kyalami in 1975. Which team was he driving for?

6. Pierfrancesco Chili won Race 1 and Race 2, when World Superbikes first visited Kyalami in 1998. What make of bike was he riding?

7. Which Swedish driver, driving a Lotus-Ford, won the 1978 Formula One Grand Prix at Kyalami?

8. Which American rider won the first race and set the fastest lap at the World Superbikes Kyalami race in the year 2000?

9. At World Superbikes race in 1999 at Kyalami, which British rider won both races?

10. The A1 Grand Prix series visited Kyalami in the 2008/2009 season. Which Swiss driver won the feature race at the circuit?

11. At the 1983 South African Grand Prix two Italians finished first and second. Riccardo Patrese won the race, but which Italian, driving for Alfa Romeo, finished second?

12. Who was the last McLaren driver to win a South African Grand Prix at Kyalami in 1984?

13. Who was the last Ferrari driver to win a South African Grand Prix at Kyalami in 1979?

14. In the 2009 World Supersport race at Kyalami, which future Irish MotoGP and World Superbike rider won the race, beating Cal Crutchlow by two and a half seconds?

15. Who was the last British driver to win a Formula One Grand Prix at Kyalami?

16. Which team was Mario Andretti driving for when he won the South African Grand Prix in 1971

17. Which German Formula One driver finished 3rd on the podium at the 1976 South African Grand Prix, driving for McLaren?

18. With records kept between 1961 and 1987, which Formula One driver holds the race lap record, set whilst he drove for Williams in 1985?

19. Which French driver won the 1980 Formula One South African Grand Prix?

20. Which British driver won the 1968 Formula One South African Grand Prix?

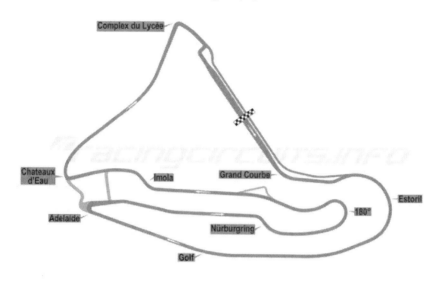

ROUND 9

CIRCUIT DE NEVERS

MAGNY-COURS

1. Jordan-Mugen-Honda won the Formula One French Grand Prix at Magny-Cours in 1999. Who was the driver?

2. Which German driver won the 2005 World Touring Car Race of France?

3. Which American rider won the 1992 500cc Motorcycle French Grand Prix?

4. Which French rider won Race 1 of the 2014 World Superbike Championship at Magny-Cours?

5. In the 2005 GP2 race at Magny-Cours, which future Formula One World Champion finished third driving for ART Grand Prix?

6. Which Formula One driver won eight times at Magny-Cours?

7. Driving for Ferrari, which driver won the 2007 Formula One French Grand Prix?

8. Which British rider won both races at the 2013 World Superbike Championship event at Magny-Cours?

9. What was the name of the British rider and future MotoGP rider who finished second in the 2009 World Supersport race at Magny-Cours?

10. What was the name of the Australian rider, on a Ducati, who won and set the fastest lap of Race 2 at the 2006 World Superbike race?

11. Who is the only Brazilian Formula One driver to win a Grand Prix at Magny-Cours?

12. Who was the winning driver in the BMW powered Williams car which won the 2003 Formula One French Grand Prix?

13. Which British rider won Race 1 of the 2004 World Superbike race at Magny-Cours?

14. Which Italian driver finished third on the podium in the 2008 French Grand Prix?

15. Damon Hill won the 1996 Formula One French Grand Prix, but which Ferrari driver was on pole position?

16. Which team was Kimi Raikkonen driving for when he finished second to Fernando Alonso at the 2005 Formula One French Grand Prix?

17. In 2010 at the World Superbike Championship races, Cal Crutchlow took Superpole, set fastest laps in both races and won Race 1. Which Italian rider stopped him from taking all the accolades by winning Race 2?

18. David Coulthard and Mika Hakkinen made it a McLaren one-two at the 2000 Formula One Grand Prix. Which Brazilian driver finished third in a Ferrari?

19. Which Spanish rider won both races and took fastest laps at the 2011 World Superbike event?

20. Which Honda driver was the only retirement at the 2008 Formula One French Grand Prix?

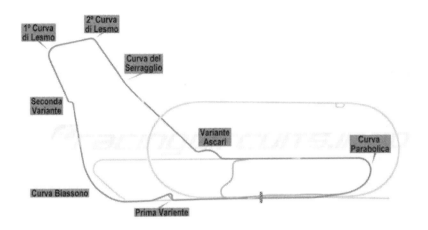

ROUND 10

AUTODROMO

NAZIONALE MONZA

1. Which American rider won the 500cc Nations Motorcycle Grand Prix in 1981 at Monza?

2. Two South American drivers won the 2004 and 2005 Italian Formula One Grand Prix's. Rubens Barrichello won in 2004, which South American driver won it in 2005?

3. Which Australian rider won the 500cc Nations Motorcycle Grand Prix in 1987?

4. Alain Prost won the 1981 Formula One Grand Prix. What team was he driving for?

5. McLaren-TAG won back-to-back Grand Prix's in 1984 and 1985. Alain Prost won in 1985, which McLaren driver won the year before?

6. Who was the first American driver to win a Formula One race at Monza?

7. The Italian Grand Prix was won by British drivers from 1956 to 1959. Stirling Moss won three of them, who was the other British driver?

8. Which Austrian driver won the 1988 Formula One Italian Grand Prix?

9. Which British rider finished third at the 1981 500c Nations Motorcycle Grand Prix?

10. Which British driver won the 1995 Formula One Italian Grand Prix?

11. Which Formula One racing team won, to date, their only Grand Prix at Monza in 2008?

12. Three American riders, all riding Yamaha's, were on the podium for the 1986 Nations Motorcycle Grand Prix. Mike Baldwin finished third, Randy Mamola finished second. Who won?

13. What is the name given to turns six and seven at Monza?

14. Which British driver, driving a Honda, won the 1967 Formula One Italian Grand Prix on the old Monza Road Circuit?

15. Juan Manuel Fangio won his first Italian Grand Prix in 1953. Which make of car was he driving?

16. Who was the first Brazilian driver to win a Formula One race at Monza?

17. Which French driver won both races in 2012 and 2013 in the World Touring Car Championship, driving a Chevrolet?

18. Which Ferrari driver won the 1979 Formula One Italian Grand Prix?

19. Which British driver won the first race of the World Touring Car Race of Italy in 2006?

20. As of 2019, which Formula One driver holds the lap record for the modern circuit at Monza, set in 2004 driving a Ferrari?

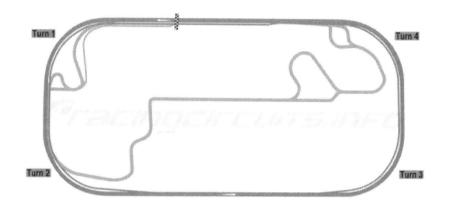

ROUND 11

INDIANAPOLIS

MOTOR SPEEDWAY

1. What is the nickname of the Indianapolis Motor Speedway?

2. What is the name of the first woman to have qualified for the Indianapolis 500?

3. Which driver won the Indianapolis 500 in the first Formula One World Championship season of 1950?

4. What was the nationality of the first non-American Indy 500 winner in 1913?

5. Indy Car have competed the Grand Prix of Indianapolis at this circuit since 2014. Which Australian driver has won this event three times?

6. Who was the first British racing driver to win the Indy 500 in 1965?

7. In what year did British driver Dario Franchitti win this third and last Indy 500?

8. In what year did the NASCAR race, the Brickyard 400, first take place at the Indianapolis Motor Speedway?

9. Which driver won the last Formula One United States Grand Prix at the Indianapolis Motor Speedway in 2007?

10. As of 2019 which driver has won the most NASCAR Brickyard 400 races, with five victories?

11. Which Indy Car and Le Mans driver won the first TUDOR Sportscar race at this circuit, partnering Alex Popow and driving a Riley Ford?

12. The MotoGP World Championship raced at Indianapolis from 2008 until 2015. Which rider had the most victories in the premier class with three wins?

13. Which Formula One team had the most success winning six races at the Indianapolis Motor Speedway?

14. Which driver won the 2016 Indy 500, as a rookie?

15. Which former Formula One driver won the Indy 500 in 2000, driving for Chip Ganassi Racing?

16. How many times did A.J. Foyt win the Indy 500?

17. Casey Stoner won the 2011 MotoGP race at Indianapolis. What make of bike was he riding?

18. Which NASCAR driver, driving for Joe Gibbs Racing, won back-to-back Brickyard 400 races in 2015 and 2016

19. Which car manufacturer, as of 2019, has won the most Brickyard 400 races, which 17 victories?

20. Who won the Formula One United States Grand Prix at Indianapolis, driving for McLaren in 2001?

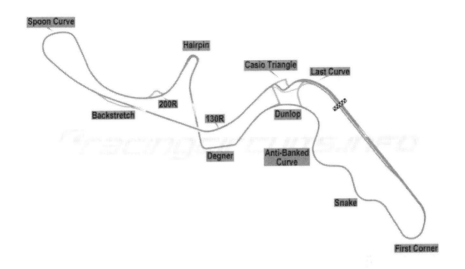

ROUND 12

SUZUKA

INTERNATIONAL

RACING COURSE

1. In what year did Formula One first race at Suzuka?

2. Who was the first British Formula One driver to win a Japanese Grand Prix at Suzuka?

3. MotoGP last featured at Suzuka in 2003. Who won that race, on a Honda?

4. Which British rider won three back-to-back Suzuka 8 Hour races from 2016-2018, riding a Yamaha?

5. After the start line, riders and drivers take turn one, then from turns two through to seven as a series of esses. They then enter the Dunlop Curve. What is the name of the section of track, directly after the Dunlop Curve?

6. Who was the first McLaren driver to win a Formula One Japanese Grand Prix at Suzuka?

7. Who was the last American rider to win a 500cc Motorcycle Grand Prix at Suzuka in 1999?

8. Which Italian Formula One driver won the 1992 Japanese Grand Prix at Suzuka?

9. Formula One driver Gerhard Berger won two Japanese Grand Prix's at Suzuka. His first was in a Ferrari, which team was he driving for when he won his second in 1991?

10. Having won the 250cc Motorcycle Grand Prix in 1996, which Italian rider went on to win the 500c race at Suzuka in 1998?

11. Which Benetton-Ford Formula One driver won the 1989 Japanese Grand Prix?

12. Which Argentinian driver won Race 1 of the World Touring Car Championship at Suzuka in 2014?

13. Which British driver won Race 2 of the World Touring Car Championship at Suzuka in 2018?

14. Which Formula One Ferrari driver won the 2003 Japanese Grand Prix?

15. Which Formula One team was Kimi Raikkonen driving for when he won the 2005 Japanese Grand Prix?

16. How many times has Alain Prost won at Suzuka in Formula One?

17. What make of bike was Wayne Rainey riding when he won the 1993 500cc Motorcycle Grand Prix at Suzuka?

18. What make of car was Gabriele Tarquini driving when he won Race 2 of the World Touring Car Championship at Suzuka in 2014?

19. Which British driver and 2006 McLaren Autsport BRDC award winner partnered Hideki Mutoh to win the GT500 at the Super GT race in 2016?

20. At the end of the 2018 season, who was the last non-Mercedes driver to win the Formula One Japanese Grand Prix?

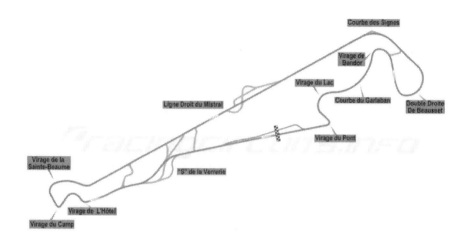

ROUND 13

CIRCUIT PAUL RICARD

1. Which other British rider teamed up with Carl Fogarty and Steve Hislop to win the 1992 Bol d'Or at Paul Ricard?

2. The 6 Hours of Castellet has been competed, on and off, at Paul Ricard since 1970. Which British driver partnered Rinaldo Capello in an Audi R15 TDI to win the race in 2010?

3. Which Formula One driver won three successive races from 1988 to 1990 at the French Grand Prix, held at Paul Ricard?

4. In what year was the first Formula One World Championship French Grand Prix held at Paul Ricard?

5. Which French driver won the first World Touring Car Championship race at Paul Ricard in 2014?

6. Which Spanish rider won the 500cc Motorcycle French Grand Prix at Paul Ricard in 1998 and 1999?

7. Which future Formula One driver would team up with Jonathan Hirschi to win the 6 Hours of Castellet driving for Murphy Prototypes in 2013?

8. Which former World Rally Champion won Race 1 of the 2015 World Touring Car Championship Race of France?

9. Which Formula One driver, driving for Lotus-Ford, won the 1973 French Grand Prix at Paul Ricard?

10. Who was the first British 500cc Motorcycle rider to win the French Grand Prix at Paul Ricard?

11. Which American rider won the 500cc Motorcycle French Grand Prix in 1984?

12. Who partnered Alain Prost and won the 1982 Formula One French Grand Prix but then switched to Ferrari for the following season?

13. After Formula One switched to Dijon for the 1984 season, they returned to Paul Ricard in 1985. Nelson Piquet won the race in the Brabham-BMW, but which Williams driver on pole did he beat by over six and half seconds to claim the victory?

14. Who was the first Williams Formula One driver to win a French Grand Prix at Paul Ricard?

15. Which Formula One driver won the 1976 French Grand Prix at Paul Ricard but was only sitting fourth in the championship at the time?

16. When Formula One returned to Paul Ricard in 2018, which driver took pole position?

17. Which driver, as of 2019, has the most World Touring Car Championship race wins at Paul Ricard?

18. Which 500cc Motorcycle grand prix rider won back-to-back races at Paul Ricard in 1996 and 1997?

19. Which British Formula One driver won the 1971 French Grand Prix?

20. Mario Andretti won the 1978 Formula One French Grand Prix at Paul Ricard, but for what team was he driving for?

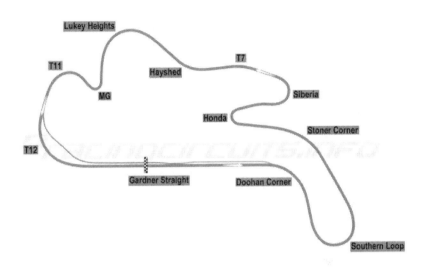

ROUND 14

PHILLIP ISLAND

GRAND PRIX CIRCUIT

1. In what year did the Superbike World Championship first race at Phillip Island?

2. Long before the Formula One World Championship was formed in 1950, Phillip Island did host Formula One racing. What was the last year it hosted a non-world championship Formula One race?

3. The Australian Supercars Championship race at Phillip Island. It was not held in 2017 or 2018, but on its return which Ford Mustang GT driver, racing for DJR Team Penske won the race in 2019?

4. Which MotoGP rider won six consecutive races at Phillip Island between 2007 and 2012?

5. Marco Melandri won the 2006 MotoGP at Phillip Island. What make of bike was he riding?

6. As of 2019, which car manufacturer has won the most Australian Supercars Championship races at Phillips Island?

7. What is name given to the straight leading down to turn one, the surname of which is dedicated to a former motorcycle racer?

8. Which British rider won race 1 at Phillip Island in the 1994 Superbike World Championship?

9. Which New Zealand driver won the 2012 Australian Supercars race at Phillip Island driving a Ford FG Falcon for the Stone Brothers Racing team?

10. The Moto2 support race was won by riders from the same country between 2012 and 2015. What country was it?

11. Who was the last British rider to win a premier class motorcycle Grand Prix at Phillip Island in MotoGP or 500cc?

12. Both races at the 2000 Superbikes World Championship event at Phillip Island were won by Australian riders. Anthony Gobert won the first race, which rider won the second race?

13. Which bike manufacturer was Valentino Rossi riding for when he won the 500cc Motorcycle Grand Prix at Phillip Island in 2001?

14. Which British rider won the opening race of the 2010 Superbikes World Championship season, riding a Suzuki?

15. Australian Supercars have been racing at Phillip Island since 1990. As of 2019 how many times has a Volvo won the race at this circuit?

16. The first time a 500cc Motorcycle Grand Prix took place at Phillip Island was in 1989. Which Honda rider won that race?

17. Which Australian rider won both Superbike World Championship races at Phillip Island in 2008?

18. Jonathan Rea won both races at Phillip Island for the 2016 Superbikes World Championship, but which other British rider took Superpole?

19. Which Yamaha rider won the 2013 MotoGP Australian Grand Prix?

20. Having won at Phillip Island in Moto3 in 2016, which rider then went on to win at the same circuit in Moto2 in 2018?

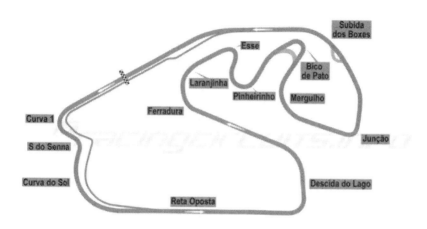

ROUND 15

AUTODROMO

JOSE CARLOS PACE

1. The Autodromo Jose Carlos Pace is also known by another name, what is it?

2. Which former Formula One driver won the 6 Hours of Sao Paulo in 2012, partnering Nicolas Lapierre for Toyota Racing?

3. Which former Formula One driver, who raced for BAR, Jordan and Toyota, won the last race of the Stock Car Brasil championship at this circuit in 2013 and 2018?

4. The first Formula One race at the circuit in 1972 was a non-championship race, but was still heavily contested by a strong driver line-up. Which Argentine Brabham driver won the race?

5. Who was the first British Formula One driver to win a Grand Prix at the circuit?

6. Which French driver teamed up with Neel Jani and Marc Lieb for Porsche in 2014 to win the 6 Hours of Sao Paulo?

7. After a break, Formula One returned to the circuit in 1990. Which Ferrari driver won the Brazilian Grand Prix that year?

8. From 1973 to 1975 the Brazilian Grand Prix was won by a Brazilian. Carlos Pace won in 1975, which driver won both the 1973 and 1974 races?

9. At the Brazilian Grand Prix's of 2014 and 2015, which driver took pole and won in both races?

10. Which Williams driver took pole and won the 1997 Brazilian Grand Prix?

11. Prior to 2019, who was the last McLaren driver to win the Brazilian Grand Prix at Interlagos?

12. A Ferrari finished on the top step of the podium from 2006 to 2008. Kimi Raikkonen won in 2007, which driver won the other two races?
13. Which driver won back-to-back Brazilian Grand Prix's at this circuit in 2004 and 2005, both for different teams?

14. How many Formula One races at this circuit did Michael Schumacher win?

15. Jordan won only one Grand Prix at this circuit, in 2003. Who was driving the car?

16. The 1979 and 1980 Formula One races were both won by French drivers. Rene Arnoux won for Renault in 1980, who won the year before driving a Ligier-Ford?

17. Who was the first Ferrari driver to win at this circuit?

18. In 2013, Audi won the 6 Hours of Sao Paulo with three drivers. Benoit Treluyer and Marcel Fassler were two, who was the third?

19. Which McLaren driver won the 1993 Brazilian Grand Prix?

20. Which driver won back-to-back Formula One races in 1998 and 1999?

ROUND 16

SNAEFELL

MOUNTAIN COURSE

1. Which rider, on an MV Augusta, won the Isle Of Man Senior TT from 1968 to 1972?

2. In what year did Joey Dunlop win his first Senior TT?

3. Who won the Senior TT in 1990, on a Honda, averaging 110.95mph?

4. In what year was the last 500cc Senior TT part of the FIM Motorcycle Grand Prix World Championship?

5. When Mike Hailwood won the Senior TT race in 1961, what make of bike was he riding?

6. From 2005 until 2007, riding a Suzuki, which New Zealand rider won the Superstock TT on all three occasions?

7. Which British rider won the Isle Of Man Senior TT in 1977?

8. Who was the last non-British or Irish rider to win the Senior TT?

9. Who has the most Lightweight TT wins with six?

10. Which sidecar marque, or manufacturer, has the most TT wins as of 2018, with 40?

11. In what year did the Zero TT first appear as an official race at the Isle of Man event?

12. Which Senior TT winner won the Zero TT in 2015?

13. Which rider won back-to-back Senior TT's in 1991 and 1992 on two different makes of bike, a Honda and a Norton?

14. In what year was the first Isle Of Man Senior TT?

15. Which rider won both Supersport TT races, two years running, in 2015 and 2016?

16. Riding a Norton, who won the Senior TT's in 1950 and 1951?

17. From 1963 to 1965, which Rhodesian rider won the 250cc and 350cc races, all in succession?

18. How many World Championship Senior TT races did John Surtees win?

19. As of 2018, who was the last Northern Irish rider to win the Senior TT?

20. From 1977 to 1984 the same make of bike won the Senior TT. What make was it?

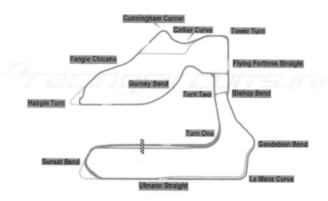

ROUND 17

SEBRING

INTERNATIONAL

RACEWAY

1. Prior to winning two DTM championships, which German driver took pole at Zandvoort DTM race in 2003?

2. The Masters of Formula Three, raced at Zandvoort, brought together drivers from various national F3 championships for an annual race. Which future British Formula One driver won this event in 1991, the first year it was held?

3. Prior to being taken off the Formula One calendar, which driver has the most race wins at the Dutch Grand Prix held at Zandvoort?

4. Before it was removed from the racing calendar, who was the last Formula One driver to win at Zandvoort in 1985, driving for McLaren?

5. Which British driver, competing for Mercedes, took pole in both DTM races, clocked the fastest lap and won Race 1 at Zandvoort in 2018?

6. Which Italian Formula One driver won the Dutch Grand Prix at Zandvoort in 1952 and 1953?

7. Who was the last future British Formula One driver to win The Masters of Formula Three event in 2006?

8. Jackie Stewart won three Formula One races at Zandvoort. His first two victories were for the Matra team, but what was his team when he won his last race at the circuit in 1973?

9. Between 1981 and 1984, the Dutch Grand Prix was won by three drivers of the same nationality, one of them winning twice. What country did they come from?

10. Who was the last non-European Formula One driver to win at Zandvoort?

11. Which Formula One constructor has the most wins at Zandvoort?

12. How many races did Niki Lauda win at Zandvoort?

13. Talbot-Lago won two non-championship Formula One races at Zandvoort in 1950 and 1951. Who was the French driver on both occasions?

14. Who was the last Australian Formula One driver to win at Zandvoort?

15. Which former Formula One driver took pole and won Race 1 in the 2017 DTM race competed at Zandvoort?

16. Which former World Rallycross champion won the DTM race at Zandvoort in 2014?

17. Max Verstappen won the The Masters of Formula Three race in 2014, but in what year did his father Jos win the same race?

18. Which current Formula One driver won back-to-back Masters of Formula Three races in 2009 and 2010?

19. In what year did Lewis Hamilton win the Masters of Formula Three race?

20. Jacky Ickx won the 1971 Dutch Grand Prix. What team was he driving for that day?

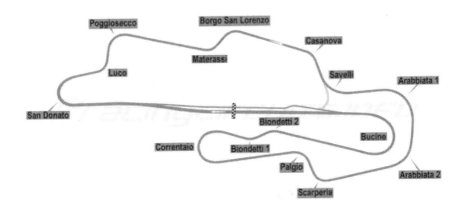

ROUND 19

MUGELLO CIRCUIT

1. In what year did the Nations Motorcycle Grand Prix first appear at Mugello?

2. Which American rider took pole and won Race 1 at the Superbike World Championship event held at Mugello in 1991?

3. Which British driver won the 2008 DTM race at Mugello?

4. Which Ducati rider won the MotoGP Italian Grand Prix at Mugello in 2017?

5. Which rider won three consecutive MotoGP Italian Grand Prix's from 2011 to 2013?

6. Which French rider took pole, set fastest laps and won both races at the Superbike World Championship event held at Mugello in 1992?

7. Prior to 2018, who was the last non-European MotoGP rider to win the Italian Grand Prix at Mugello?

8. Which future MotoGP champion won the 125cc class race at Mugello in 1997?

9. Which racing series was supposed to open the 2008/09 season at Mugello but cancelled due to the delay in building new chassis for race cars?

10. At the 2018 MotoGP Italian Grand Prix, Ducati finished first and second on the podium. Which bike manufacturer finished third?

11. In the top class of Motorcycle Grand Prix racing, who was the last American rider to win the Nations Grand Prix at Mugello?

12. What year was the first Motorcycle Grand Prix event where the race at Mugello was no longer known as the Nations Grand Prix and was renamed the Italian Grand Prix?

13. Which British MotoGP rider won the 125cc race at Mugello in 2009?

14. Dani Pedrosa won the 2010 Italian Grand Prix for the Repsol Honda Team, but who was his team mate who finished third on the podium?

15. Valentino Rossi won seven consecutive Italian Grand Prix's at Mugello from 2002 until 2008. Which rider was the last to win the race prior to the Rossi streak of victories?

16. Which Yamaha rider won the 1978 Nations Grand Prix at Mugello?

17. Which Italian rider won three consecutive 250cc races at Mugello from 1995 to 1997?

18. In 2008, which Italian rider won the 250cc race at Mugello?

19. Prior to 2018, who was the last British rider to win a Moto2 race at Mugello?

20. Out of the three Spanish riders, Jorge Lorenzo, Dani Pedrosa and Marc Marquez, who has the most race wins across all three class of Grand Prix Motorcycle racing at Mugello?

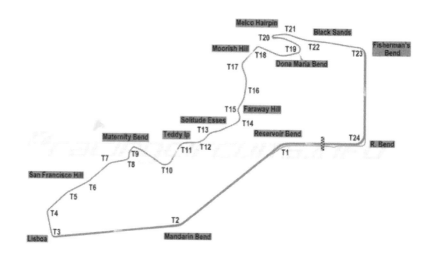

ROUND 20

GUIA CIRCUIT

1. What is the name of the first turn after the start at the Guia Circuit?

2. As of 2019, which former British rider holds the Motorcycle Grand Prix lap record, which he set on a Kawasaki Ninja ZX-10R in 2010?

3. Augusto Farfus won the FIA GT World Cup at the Guia Circuit in 2018. What make of car was he driving?

4. Prior to 2018, the last non-British winner of the Motorcycle Grand Prix at Guia was Andreas Hofmann in 1997. What country is Andreas Hofmann from?

5. Which British touring car driver holds the record for most touring car wins at the Guia Circuit, with eight?

6. The main race or title race is for Formula Three drivers. Which future Formula One German driver won this race in 1995?

7. Which former GP3 Series, DTM and Formula E driver won the main race in 2012?

8. Which driver, famed for his drives for Toyota at the 24 Hours of Le Mans, won the main race in 2006?

9. Which motorcycle world champion won the Motorcycle Grand Prix at Guia in 1992?

10. As of 2019, which British rider holds the record for the most wins at the Motorcycle Grand Prix at the Guia Circuit?

11. Driving a Ford Sierra RS500, which British Touring Car driver won the event at Guia in 1989?

12. Which Formula E driver and winner of the Nurburgring 24 Hour race won the GT Cup at the Guia Circuit in 2014 and 2015, driving a Mercedes-Benz SLS AMG GT3?

13. Famed road racer Ian Hutchinson won the motorcycle event in 2013. What make of bike was he riding?

14. Which European driver, who went on to compete in IndyCar won the main race at Guia in 2014 and 2015?

15. Which British driver won back-to-back main races in 2017 and 2018?

16. Which Formula E and World Endurance Championship driver and former GP3 Series champion won the main race in 2013?

17. Mehdi Bennani and Robert Huff won races one and two respectively at the Guia Circuit in 2017, but what make of touring car were they both driving?

18. How many times has two-time British Touring Car champion Alain Menu won the touring car event at Guia?

19. Which Isle of Man Senior TT winner won the motorcycle event in 2001?

20. Ayrton Senna won the main race at the Guia Circuit once. In what year did he take the victory?

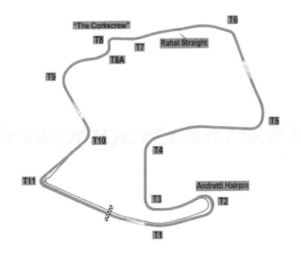

ROUND 21

LAGUNA SECA

RACEWAY

1. What is the name of the plunging, downhill signature turn at Laguna Seca?

2. The last United States Motorcycle Grand Prix was held at Laguna Seca in 2013. Who won the MotoGP race?

3. Which Italian racing driver won the CART/Champ Car Series Monterey Grand Prix at Laguna Seca in 1996 for Chip Ganassi Racing?

4. Which British rider won Race 1 of the Superbike World Championship at Laguna Seca in 2013?

5. Which MotoGP rider, on a Honda, won the 2009 United States Motorcycle Grand Prix?

6. Tequila Patron ESM won the Continental Tire Monterey Grand Prix, part of the IMSA WeatherTech SportsCar, Championship in 2018. Johannes van Overbeek was one driver, but who was his Brazilian team mate?

7. Which British rider won both World Superbike races at Laguna Seca in 2017?

8. Which Australian rider set fastest laps and won both races at the World Superbike race in 2004?

9. Which future Formula One World Champion won both races of the 1993 Toyota Atlantic Championship at Laguna Seca in 1993?

10. What was the name of the Canadian racing driver who won back-to-back CART/Champ Car Series Monterey Grand Prix's in 2003 and 2004?

11. Which American rider won back-to-back MotoGP races in 2005 and 2006?

12. What was the name of the German driver, the son and nephew of two Formula One drivers, who was part of the Audi Sport Team Magnus who won the California 8 Hours in 2017?

13. Which British rider won both World Superbike races at Laguna Seca in 2015?

14. What was the name of the Brazilian IndyCar driver who won the Monterey Grand Prix in the year 2000?

15. What future Formula One champion won the Formula 5000 race at Laguna Seca in 1975?

16. Which British racing driver won back-to-back USAC Road Racing Championship races at Laguna Seca in 1960 and 1961 in a Lotus 19-Climax?

17. Bruce McLaren raced in the Can-Am Championship at Laguna Seca driving his McLaren M8B-Chevrolet. How many times was he a race winner?

18. At the 2002 World Superbike round held at Laguna Seca, Troy Bayliss won the first race. Which American rider won the second race for Castrol Honda?

19. Which multiple American CART/Champ Car Series champion won four consecutive Monterey Grand Prix's from 1984 to 1987?

20. The first United States Motorcycle Grand Prix was held at Laguna Seca in 1988. Which American rider won the 500cc race?

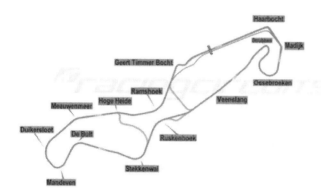

ROUND 22

TT CIRCUIT ASSEN

1. The TT Circuit Assen first appeared on the British Superbike Championship calendar in 2012. Which rider won the first ever championship race of that year?

2. Riding a Honda, which rider won the MotoGP race at Assen in 2016?

3. Which future Spanish MotoGP rider won the Moto3 race at Assen in 2012?

4. Which British motorcycle rider has the most Grand Prix wins in all classes at Assen?

5. Jonathan Rea won both World Superbike races at Assen in 2016, but which fellow British rider took Superpole for the event?

6. In 2013, Alex Lowes grabbed pole, set the fastest lap and won Race 1 at Assen. What make of bike was he riding?

7. Valentino Rossi won the 2017 Dutch TT at Assen, but which Octo Pramac Racing rider, on a Ducati, was second in this MotoGP race?

8. Which British rider gained pole position for the 2014 British Superbike race at Assen?

9. At the 2012 MotoGP race held at Assen, the two Repsol Honda riders finished first and second. Dani Pedrosa was the rider in second, who won the race?

10. Which Milwaukee Yamaha rider gained pole, set fastest laps and won both 2015 British Superbike races at Assen?

11. Which British rider won both World Superbike races at Assen in 2015?

12. Which Ducati rider finished second to Marc Marquez in the 2014 MotoGP race at Assen?

13. The CHAMP Car World Series race at Assen in 2007 was won by which British driver?

14. Which British rider took Superpole for the 2018 World Superbike race at Assen?

15. Which British rider won both British Superbike races at Assen in 2016?

16. Which French MotoGP rider won the Moto2 race at Assen in 2015?

17. Who was the last American to win a premier class Motorcycle Grand Prix at Assen?

18. In the 2017 British Superbike Championship, Sylvain Guintoli won the second race of the weekend. What make of bike was he riding?

19. Who was the last British rider to win a premier class Motorcycle Grand Prix at Assen?

20. Which of these riders has the most wins in all classes at Assen for Motorcycle Grand Prix racing? Valentino Rossi, Giacomo o Agostini or Mick Doohan?

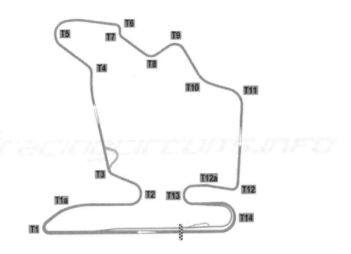

ROUND 23

HUNGARORING

1. The first time a world championship Formula One race was held at this circuit was in 1986. Which Williams driver won that race?

2. At the 2011 World Touring Car Championship Race of Hungary, two Chevrolet drivers won both races. Alain Menu won the first race, but which French driver won the second race?

3. The Hungarian Motorcycle Grand Prix was only held twice at this circuit. When it was first raced in 1990 which Honda rider won the 500cc race?

4. The second Hungarian Motorcycle Grand Prix was held in 1992. Riding a Cagiva bike, which American rider won the 500cc race?

5. Which former Jordan Formula One driver won Race 1 of the World Touring Car race at the Hungaroring in 2017?

6. Marco Wittman won the DTM race at the Hungaroring in 2014. What make of car was he driving?

7. Across all classes which bike manufacturer has the most Motorcycle Grand Prix wins at the Hungaroring, with three victories?

8. As of 2018, which Formula One driver has the most Grand Prix wins at this circuit, with six?

9. As of 2018 which Formula One constructor has the most wins, with eleven?

10. Up until 2018, who was the last non-European Formula One driver to win the Hungarian Grand prix?

11. Jenson Button won two Hungarian Grand Prix's. One was with McLaren in 2011, but which other constructor did he taste victory with at this circuit?

12. Who was the first British Formula One driver to win at the Hungaroring?

13. Which Williams driver won the 1990 Hungarian Grand Prix?

14. Ayrton Senna won the 1988 Hungarian Grand Prix. His McLaren team mate came second. What was his name?

15. At the 1994 Hungarian Grand Prix, with a fourth place, who was the highest placed McLaren driver for that race?

16. At the 1995 Hungarian Grand Prix, three Renault powered cars finished on the podium. Damon Hill and David Coulthard finished first and second for Williams, which driver finished third?

17. Michael Schumacher won three races at the Hungaroring for Ferrari. Rubens Barrichello was his team mate for two of those victories, who was the other driver when Michael won his first Hungarian Grand Prix for Ferrari in 1998?

18. How many times was Damon Hill a winner at the Hungarian Grand Prix?

19. In what year did Jacques Villeneuve win his first of two Hungarian Grand Prix's for Williams?

20. For the 2008 Hungarian Grand Prix, Lewis Hamilton took pole position in his McLaren. He finished fifth in the race but what was the name of his McLaren team mate who won the only Grand Prix of his Formula One career

ROUND 24

NURBURGRING

1. After his victory in the 1968 German Grand Prix, which Formula One driver nicknamed the Nordschleife, "The Green Hell"?

2. The European Grand Prix was first held at the Nurburgring in 1984. Which McLaren driver won that race?

3. The last European Grand Prix at the Nurburgring took place in 2007. Which McLaren driver won that race?

4. Before switching to the Sachsenring, the German Motorcycle Grand Prix was held at the Nurburgring. Who was the last 500cc rider to win at the circuit on a Honda in 1997?

5. Hans-Joachim Stuck and Clemens Schickentanz won the first ever 24 Hours Nurburgring driving a BMW for the Koepchen BMW Tuning team. In what year was this?

6. In 1973, which future Formula One world champion won the 24 Hours Nurburgring, partnering Hans-Peter Joisten in a BMW?

7. The Luxembourg Grand Prix was held twice at the Nurburgring. Which Formula One driver won the first Luxembourg Grand Prix in 1997, driving for Williams?

8. After the German Grand Prix was held at the Hockenheimring from 1977 until 1984, it returned to this circuit in 1985. Which Ferrari driver won that race?

9. Which British Formula One driver won the 1999 European Grand Prix at the Nurburgring for Stewart-Ford?

10. Prior to 2018, who was the last British Formula One driver to win a German Grand Prix at the Nurburgring?

11. Which Ferrari driver won the 1974 German Grand Prix at the Nurburgring?

12. As a Formula One world championship race, the German Grand Prix was raced at the Nurburgring from 1951 until it moved to Berlin for 1959. During this time it was won by four Ferrari drivers, Tony Brooks, Juan Manuel Fangio, Alberto Ascari and Giuseppe Farina. Which one of those drivers won it the most times during that period in a Ferrari?

13. Who was the last Formula One driver to win a world championship race on the old Nordschleife circuit?

14. In 2016 Maro Engel, Bernd Schneider, Adam Christodoulou and Manuel Metzger all teamed up to win the 24 Hours Nurburgring, but which make of car were they driving?

15. The last Luxembourg Grand Prix was held at the Nurburgring in 1998. Which McLaren driver won that race?

16. Who was the Williams driver who won the 2003 European Grand Prix at the Nurburgring?

17. Rubens Barrichello won the European Grand Prix twice, but only once at the Nurburgring. What team was he driving for when he claimed that victory?

18. Driving a Brabham-Ford, which six time 24 Hours of Le Mans winner won the Formula One German Grand Prix in 1969?

19. Between 1961 and 1965, four different British Formula One drivers won the German Grand Prix at the Nurburgring. John Surtees won twice, Jim Clark and Stirling Moss were also victors, but who was the other British driver?

20. Mark Webber won the 2009 German Grand Prix at the Nurburgring. Which Brawn-Mercedes driver finished second?

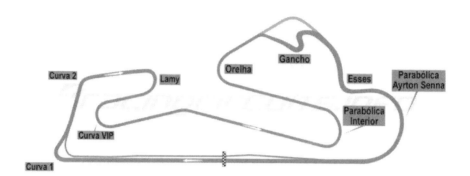

ROUND 25

AUTODROMO

DO ESTORIL

1. Which former Formula E champion took pole position at Round 3 of the 2005/06 A1GP championship at Estoril?

2. Which 24 Hours of Le Mans LMP2 class winning British driver won the 4 Hours of Estoril alongside Giedo van der Garde and Simon Dolan for the G-Drive Racing team in 2016?

3. Which ex-Formula One driver took two World Touring Car Race of Portugal wins at Estoril in 2009 and 2010?

4. Which MotoGP rider won the Portuguese Motorcycle Grand Prix in 2008, 2009 and 2010?

5. Turn 13 or the Parabolica at Estoril is named after which Formula One world champion?

6. Which Formula One driver has the most race wins at Estoril with three, from 1984 to 1996?

7. Who was the last British driver, prior to 2018, to win a World Touring Car race at Estoril?

8. At the 1996 Formula One Portuguese Grand Prix points were given to the top six drivers. Four of these drove Renault powered cars. Williams was one team, what was the other constructor with a Renault powered engine?

9. Which German rider won the Moto2 race at Estoril two years in succession in 2010 and 2011?

10. From 2011 until 2013 the World Touring Car Race of Portugal were won by the same make of car. What make was it?

11. Which Formula One constructor is the most successful at Estoril with six race wins?

12. Nigel Mansell won the 1992 Portuguese Grand Prix, but who was his Williams team mate who finished second in the race?

13. Valentino Rossi won the Portuguese Motorcycle Grand Prix on four occasions from 2001 to 2004. He won three times on a Honda, but what make of bike did he ride for the fourth victory?

14. Which MotoGP rider won the last Portuguese Motorcycle Grand Prix at Estoril on a Honda in 2012?

15. From 1994 until 1996, three Williams drivers won the Formula One Portuguese Grand Prix. Jacques Villeneuve and David Coulthard were two, who was the other driver?

16. Which Ferrari Formula One driver won the 1989 Portuguese Grand Prix?

17. Which Honda rider won the 2011 MotoGP at Estoril?

18. In 2018 Yvan Muller and Mat'o Homola won Races 1 and 3 at Estoril. What make of car were they driving?

19. Two German drivers competed in the Formula One Portuguese Grand Prix of 1995, Michael Schumacher and which other German driver, who was racing for Sauber?

20. Nigel Mansell won three Portuguese Grand Prix's. He won two for Williams, but with what other team did he win his other race at Estoril?

ROUND 26

CIRCUIT

GILLES VILLENEUVE

1. Which British racing driver won the Champ Car Grand Prix of Montreal at this circuit in 2002?

2. In 1990 the 480km of Montreal was raced at this circuit as the eighth round of the World Sportscar Championship. The race was won by Team Sauber Mercedes, but in second place was Nissan, a car driven by two British drivers. Julian Bailey was one, but which ex-Formula One driver was the other member of the team?

3. The Formula One Canadian Grand Prix first appeared at Circuit Gilles Villeneuve in 1982. Which Brabham-BMW driver won that race?

4. Rene Arnoux won the 1983 Formula One Canadian Grand Prix. He was one of two French drivers for Ferrari that season, who was the other driver who finished third in the race?

5. The Wall of Champions at Turn 14 is so called after three former Formula One World Drivers' Champions found the wall in the 1999 Canadian Grand Prix. Damon Hill and Jacques Villeneuve were two, who was the third?

6. After L'Epingle (the tight hairpin) and turns eleven and twelve, what is the name of the long straight down to turns thirteen and fourteen onto the start/finish straight?

7. Which BMW-Sauber driver won the 2008 Canadian Grand Prix?

8. Prior to 2018, who was the last Williams driver to win the Canadian Grand Prix at this circuit?

9. Ferrari finished first and second at the 1985 Formula One Canadian Grand Prix. Michele Alboreto won the race, but who was his team mate who finished second?

10. At the 1988 Canadian Grand Prix there were four British drivers involved in the race. Julian Bailey, Nigel Mansell, Derek Warwick and Jonathan Palmer. Which of these drivers finished sixth to collect the last point on offer for the race?

11. Michael Schumacher won the 1994 Grand Prix for Benetton-Ford. Who was his Scandinavian team mate, who won the 24 Hours of Le Mans twice, who finished sixth in the race?

12. Michael Schumacher led most of the 1995 Canadian Grand Prix in his Benetton until an electrical problem forced him into the pits. Which Ferrari driver took the lead and eventually won the race in difficult conditions?

13. Mika Hakkinen won the 1999 Canadian Grand Prix in a McLaren, with Benetton's Giancarlo Fisichella in second. Which Ferrari driver finished third to complete the podium?

14. Which McLaren driver won the 2005 Canadian Grand Prix?

15. Alain Prost won the 1993 Canadian Grand Prix for Williams. Who was his team mate who finished second?

16. Andrea de Cesaris finished just off the podium at the 1991 Canadian Grand Prix. Which team was he driving for in this race?

17. At the 2018 Canadian Grand Prix Brendon Hartley and which other driver were involved in a collision at turn five on the first lap which forced both their retirements from the race?

18. Which driver, who pitted six times and went from last place on lap thirty-seven after a collision, eventually won the 2011 Canadian Grand Prix?

19. Which two-time winner of the 24 Hours of Le Mans finished third on the podium at the 2007 Canadian Grand Prix, driving for Williams?

20. Who won the 1997 Canadian Grand Prix?

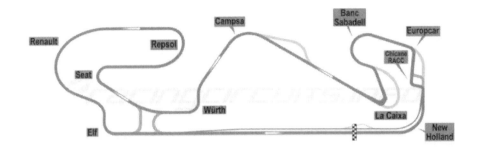

ROUND 27

CIRCUIT DE

BARCELONA-
CATALUNYA

1. Which World Rallycross driver won the first World RX of Barcelona in 2015?

2. When did the first Catalan Motorcycle Grand Prix take place at this circuit?

3. Which Williams driver won the first two Formula One Grand Prix's at this circuit in 1991 and 1992?

4. Which former DTM and World Rallycross champion won the World RX of Barcelona in 2016 and 2017?

5. Three Honda riders won the 500cc Catalan Motorcycle Grand Prix for four years from 1996 until 1999. Carlos Checa and Alex Criville both won one each, but which Honda rider won the other two in 1997 and 1998?

6. How many Spanish Grand Prix's did Ayrton Senna win at this circuit?

7. Which driver won the World RX of Barcelona in 2018?

8. Two British drivers finished on the podium of the 1994 Formula One Spanish Grand Prix. Damon Hill won, but which driver finished third in a Tyrrell?

9. From 2010 until 2018 only two Italian riders won the MotoGP Catalan Motorcycle Grand Prix. Valentino Rossi was one of them, who was the other?

10. In the 2016 World RX of Barcelona all four qualifying heats were won by Swedish drivers. Johan Kristoffersson won two, Mattias Ekstrom won another. Who was the other Swedish driver to win Qualifying 1?

11. From 2015 until 2018 all bar one of the qualifying heats has been won by a Norwegian or Swedish driver. The only other nationality to win a heat came from Finland. What was the name of the driver in Qualifying 2 of the 2017 event?

12. Apart from Petter Solberg, who was the other Norwegian driver to win a Qualifying heat at Barcelona?

13. Lois Capirossi won the MotoGP 2003 Catalan Motorcycle Grand Prix. What make of bike was he riding?

14. Which British rider won the 2015 Moto3 race at Barcelona?

15. Prior to 2018 who was the last Yamaha rider to win a MotoGP race at Barcelona?

16. Which Formula One driver won three successive Spanish Grand Prix's from 1998 to 2000?

17. Prior to 2019, who was the last Red Bull driver to win the Formula One Spanish Grand Prix?

18. Which Williams driver won the 2012 Formula One Spanish Grand Prix?

19. Ferrari won the 2007 and 2008 Formula One Spanish Grand Prix's. Kimi Raikkonen won in 2008 but which Ferrari driver won the year before?

20. Michael Schumacher raced at Barcelona for both Ferrari and Benetton during his career and won six times at this circuit. How many of those victories were for the Benetton team?

ROUND 28

CIRCUIT DE MONACO

1. Which Formula One driver won the first World Championship Monaco Grand Prix in 1950?

2. The Formula E Monaco ePrix first appeared on the calendar in 2015. Which e.dams Renault driver won that race?

3. Which future Formula One world champion finished third for ART Grand Prix in the 2005 GP2 Series race at Monaco?

4. Prior to 2019, which Formula One driver has the most race wins at Monaco with six?

5. In the 2009 GP2 Series races at Monaco, two future Formula One drivers won both races. Pastor Maldonado won Race 2, but which French driver won Race 1?

6. Which former Formula One driver won the 2019 Formula E race at Monaco for the Techeetah-DS team?

7. Which former McLaren Young Driver and Formula Renault champion won the 2017 Formula 2 sprint race at Monaco?

8. Which Formula One driver took pole and won the 2018 Monaco Grand Prix?

9. Fernando Alonso won two races at the Monaco Grand Prix. One was with Renault, but which team was he driving for when he claimed his other victory?

10. How many times did Nico Rosberg win the Monaco Grand Prix?

11. As of 2019, who is the most successful British Formula One driver at Monaco, with five victories?

12. The 1996 Monaco Grand Prix was dogged by rain. Only seven cars were officially classified as finishing, but which Ligier-Mugen-Honda driver surprisingly won the race?

13. What team was Ayrton Senna driving for when he won his first Monaco Grand Prix in 1987?

14. Who was the first British driver to win a Formula One World Championship race at Monaco?

15. Which future Sauber, McLaren and Force India driver won the 2010 GP2 Series feature race and set the fastest lap at Monaco?

16. Which former German Formula One driver, competing for Mahindra Racing, finished third in the 2017 Formula E race at Monaco?

17. Brabham, as a team, won twice at Monaco in Formula One. Riccardo Patrese won in 1987, but which New Zealand driver won their first Grand Prix in 1967?

18. In what year did Gilles Villeneuve win the Formula One Monaco Grand Prix?

19. Jenson Button won the 2009 Monaco Grand Prix for Brawn-Mercedes. Who was his team mate who finished second?

20. Which Red Bull driver won the 2010 Monaco Grand Prix?

ROUND 29

DONINGTON PARK

1. World Touring Cars moved from Brands Hatch to Donington Park in 2011. Which Chevrolet driver won both races?

2. The 1992 500km of Donington, the fourth race of the FIA Sportscar World Championship, was won by the Peugeot-Talbot team of Philippe Alliot and which other driver, who raced in Formula One for Alfa Romeo and Arrows?

3. Which British rider set a lap record of 1:27.071 at the 2015 Superbike World Championship round held at Donington?

4. The 2006 MotoGP British Grand Prix was held at Donington Park. Dani Pedrosa won the race, but who was his Italian team mate who finished third?

5. The second race of the 2013 Auto GP event held at Donington Park was won by which former Formula One Jordan test driver and HRT race driver?

6. At the 1993 Formula One European Grand Prix there were five British drivers involved. Mark Blundell, Damon Hill, Derek Warwick and Martin Brundle were four, who was the fifth?

7. Ayrton Senna won the 1993 European Grand Prix at Donington, but which Williams driver was on pole position for that race?

8. Which Japanese rider, competing for Buildbase BMW, won both British Superbike races at Donington in 2014?

9. At the 2012 British Touring Car round held at Donington, which Honda Yuasa driver won two of the three races?

10. In 2012 at the British GT event held at Donington Park, which Formula One team owner partnered Alvaro Parente to win the GT3 class?

11. Donington Park saw the opening rounds of the 2017 British Superbike Championship. Which rider took pole position and won both races, but did not win the title that year?

12. Which British Touring Car Championship driver gained pole, set the fastest lap and won Race 2 for Team BMR in 2015?

13. In The Showdown held at Donington in 2016 for the British Superbike title, which rider set both fastest laps and won both races?

14. Which Ducati rider won the 2007 MotoGP British Grand Prix?

15. Which American MotoGP rider, riding for the Monster Yamaha Tech 3 team, finished second to Andrea Dovizioso at the 2009 British Grand Prix?

16. At the 1993 Formula One European Grand Prix, there were three Brazilian drivers in the race. Ayrton Senna and Rubens Barrichello were two, but who was the third Brazilian driver for the Minardi-Ford team?

17. At the 2010 British Touring Car rounds held at Donington, two of the three races were won by Honda drivers Matt Neal and Gordon Shedden. Which Team Aon driver, driving a Ford Focus, won the other race?

18. Which Tyco Suzuki rider took the clean sweep of pole position, two fastest laps and both race wins at the Donington rounds of the 2012 British Superbike season?

19. At the 2005 MotoGP British Grand Prix, which Suzuki rider finished second to Valentino Rossi?

20. Who was Ayrton Senna's McLaren team mate for the 1993 European Grand Prix?

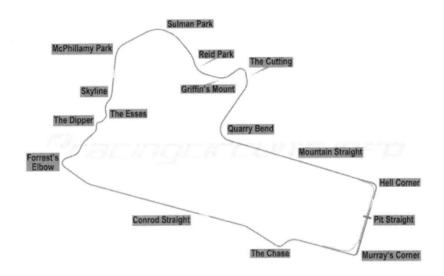

ROUND 30

MOUNT PANORAMA

1. What is the name of the last corner at Mount Panorama before entering the Pit Straight?

2. Which rider won the Australian Motorcycle Grand Prix at this circuit in 1988, riding a Yamaha?

3. Who was the last non-Australian or New Zealand driver to win the Bathurst 1000 in the same year he became 1998 British Touring Car champion?

4. Which car manufacturer has won the most Bathurst 1000 races?

5. What is the section of track called after Forrest's Elbow?

6. As of 2019, which car manufacturer has won the most Bathurst 12 Hour races?

7. Which make of car were Alvaro Parente, Shane van Gisbergen and Jonathon Webb driving when they won the 2016 Bathurst 12 Hour for Tekno Autosports?

8. Which former Finnish Formula One driver won the Bathurst 12 Hour with Craig Lowndes, Peter Edwards and John Bowe in 2014?

9. Which former Australian Formula One driver won the 1997 Bathurst 1000 with his brother Geoff in a BMW 320i?

10. In what year was the Bathurst 12 Hour first held?

11. In what year was the Bathurst 1000 first held?

12. In 2014 a trophy was introduced for the fastest time in qualifying at the Bathurst 12 Hour. Which late sportscar driver who was tragically killed at Le Mans is this trophy named after?

13. Prior to 2018, what was the last Japanese car make to win the Bathurst 12 Hour?

14. For the 2018 and 2019 Bathurst 12 Hour races they were won by a German make of car. Audi was one, which was the other?

15. What is the name of the corner directly after the main pit straight at Mount Panorama?

16. With nine victories between 1972 and 1987 in the Bathurst 1000, which driver has the nickname King Of The Mountain?

17. Which Australian Supercars racing driver has won three Bathurst 1000 races driving a Ford Falcon and four driving a Holden Commodore?

18. Which Australian Supercars racing driver and winner of most championships has won the Bathurst 1000 on four occasions?

19. Which Canadian born Hong Kong racing driver who is the 2015 GT Asia Series and two time Porsche Carrera Cup Asia champion and who has competed in the World Touring Championship, DTM and the FIA World Endurance championship has won back-to-back Bathurst 12 Hour races in 2011 and 2012 driving and Audi R8?

20. Which Japanese car make won the first ever Bathurst 12 Hour?

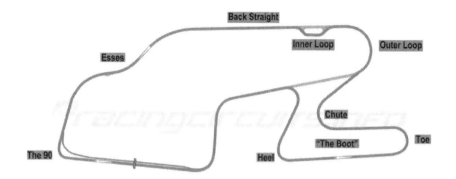

ROUND 31

WATKINS GLEN

1. The Go Bowling at The Glen is a 90 lap NASCAR Cup Series race held at this circuit. Prior to the 2019 season, which driver has the most victories in this race with five wins?

2. The 6 Hours of The Glen is a race part of the WeatherTech SportsCar Championship in the United States. In 2017 Joao Barbosa, Christian Fittipaldi and Filipe Albuquerque won the race for the Mustang Sampling Racing team. Which make of car were they driving?

3. The Grand Prix at The Glen was an IndyCar series race held at the circuit. Only two American drivers won this race as an IndyCar series race, Alexander Rossi won it in 2017 but who was the other American driver in 2008?

4. The Formula One United States Grand Prix moved to Watkins Glen in 1961. Which charismatic British driver, driving for Lotus, won the race?

5. Chase Elliott won the 2018 NASCAR race at Watkins Glen. What make of car was he driving for Hendrick Motorsports?

6. In 1972 two Formula One drivers teamed up to win the 6 Hours of The Glen in a Ferrari. Jacky Ickx was one of the drivers, but which American did he partner for the win?

7. Which New Zealand IndyCar driver was the most successful with four race wins at the Grand Prix at The Glen?

8. The Tyrrell-Ford team won back-to-back United States Grand Prix's at Watkins Glen in 1971 and 1972. Jackie Stewart won the race in 1972 but who was his French team mate who won the previous year?

9. Which former Formula One driver won the 2010 NASCAR race at Watkins Glen, driving a Chevrolet for the Earnhardt Ganassi Racing team?

10. Which British sportscar driver teamed up with American Al Holbert to win back-to-back races at the 6 Hours of The Glen in 1985 and 1986, driving a Porsche 962 for the Holbert Racing team?

11. In the IndyCar Grand Prix at The Glen which engine manufacturer is the most successful having supplied six race winning teams?

12. Formula One last raced at Watkins Glen in 1980. Who was the last British Formula One driver to win a United States Grand Prix at the circuit?

13. Who was the last Ferrari Formula One driver to win a United States Grand Prix at Watkins Glen?

14. Which Joe Gibbs Racing driver won the 2016 NASCAR race at Watkins Glen?

15. Which March-Ford Formula One driver for the 1971 season raced and won the 6 Hours of The Glen in the same year, teaming up with Andrea de Adamich for the Autodelta SpA team in an Alfa Romeo T33?

16. Niki Lauda won the 1975 United States Grand Prix but which fellow Austrian won the same race at the circuit in 1969?

17. Which former German Formula One driver who raced for teams such as Surtees, Brabham, Hesketh and Arrows won the 6 Hours Of The Glen with Manfred Schurti in 1976?

18. Alan Jones won the last United States Grand Prix at Watkins Glen. He was driving for Williams and won the championship that season, but who was his team mate?

19. Graham Hill won three successive United States Grand Prix's at Watkins Glen from 1963 to 1965, but which constructor was he driving for on all three occasions?

20. James Hunt finished third at the 1974 United States Grand Prix behind Brabham drivers Carlos Reutemann and Carlos Pace. Which Formula One team was James Hunt driving for in this race?

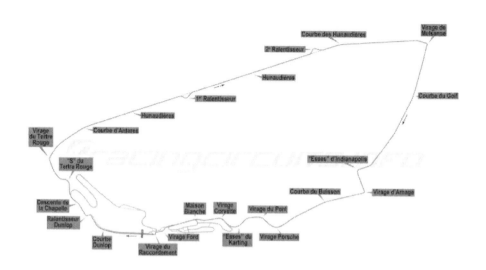

ROUND 32

CIRCUIT

DE LA SARTHE

THE 24 QUESTIONS

OF

LE MANS

1. With five victories spanning from 1975 to 1987, who is the most successful winning British driver at Le Mans with five victories?

2. Which car manufacturer has the most 24 Hour of Le Mans wins, as of 2019, with 19 victories?

3. Who is the most successful winning driver at the Circuit de la Sarthe, with nine 24 Hour of Le Mans victories and is affectionately known as "Mr. Le Mans"?

4. What is the name of the corner after "Indianapolis" at the Circuit de la Sarthe?

5. Prior to 2018, who was the last British driver to be in a winning 24 Hours of Le Mans car?

6. Prior to 2018, who was the last German driver to be in a winning 24 Hours of Le Mans car?

7. At the 2018 24 Hours of Le Mans, which make of car won the LMGTE Pro class?

8. In recent years, three Swiss drivers have won the 24 Hours of Le Mans. Sebastien Buemi and Marcel Fassler are two, who is the third?

9. The United Kingdom has produced the most winning drivers of the 24 Hours of Le Mans, with 32. What nation is the second most successful with 29 drivers?

10. How many times did Jacky Ickx win the 24 Hours of Le Mans?

11. Which of these manufacturers has won the most 24 Hours of Le Mans? - Aston Martin, Peugeot, Mercedes-Benz or Alfa Romeo?

12. The first overall win at the 24 Hours of Le Mans for Ford came in 1966 when the Ford GT40 Mk. II won the race. Chris Amon was one of the drivers, who was the other?

13. Tom Kristensen won his first 24 Hours of Le Mans in 1997 for the Joest Racing team. He teamed up with two Formula One drivers. Stefan Johansson was one, but who was the third driver from Italy?

14. Which British Formula One driver teamed up with Volker Weidler and Bertrand Gachot to the win the 24 Hours of Le Mans in a Mazda 787B?

15. Which Formula One world champion won the 24 Hours of Le Mans in 1972, driving a Matra-Simca MS670 with Frenchman Henri Pescarolo?

16. Prior to 2018, who was the last American driver to win the 24 Hours of Le Mans?

17. Vern Schuppan, Al Holbert and Hurley Haywood were the last driver line-up, prior to 2018, to have won Le Mans where there were no European drivers in the winning team. They won for Rothmans Porsche, but what year was this?

18. Toyota won the 2018 24 Hours of Le Mans, but prior to this the overall race win had been dominated by German manufacturers. What was the last non-German car manufacturer, with the exception of Toyota, to have won the race?

19. Which British car manufacturer won the 2003 24 Hours of Le Mans?

20. Who was the last driver to have won the 24 Hours of Le Mans whilst still active and competing in Formula One?

21. What is the name of the corner prior to cars speeding down the Mulsanne Straight?

22. Apart from not being contested between 1940 and 1948 due to World War Two and the reconstruction of France, what is the only year the race never took place due to a workers strike?

23. Which Formula One World Champion won the 24 Hours of Le Mans in 1955 driving with Ivor Bueb in a Jaguar D-Type?

24. Which driver won the 24 Hours of Le Mans and the Formula One World Championship in the same year, for Ferrari in 1961?

QUIZ PRIX

ANSWERS

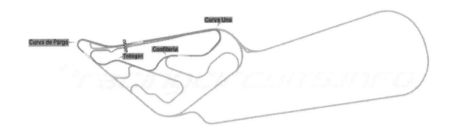

ROUND 1 – ANSWERS

AUTODROMO

JUAN Y OSCAR GALVEZ

ROUND 1 – AUTODROMO JUAN Y OSCAR GALVEZ

1. ALBERTO ASCARI

2. KENNY ROBERTS JR.

3. STIRLING MOSS

4. FERRARI

5. FERRARI

6. VALENTINO ROSSI

7. DAMON HILL

8. WILLIAMS

9. MICK DOOHAN

10. JODY SCHECKTER

11. NELSON PIQUET

12. PHIL HILL

13. EDDIE LAWSON

14. JACQUES VILLENEUVE

15. FORD

16. PORSCHE

17. JACQUES LAFFITE

18. JUAN MANUEL FANGIO

19. MARCO MELANDRI

20. ALAN JONES

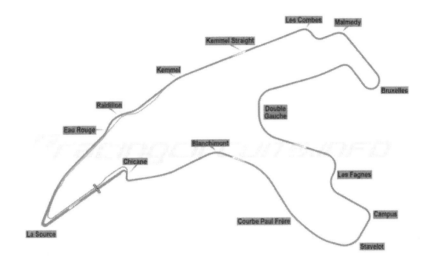

ROUND 2 – ANSWERS

CIRCUIT DE

SPA-FRANCORCHAMPS

ROUND 2 – CIRCUIT DE SPA-FRANCORCHAMPS

1. MATTIAS EKSTROM

2. 1994

3. JOHNNY HERBERT

4. AYRTON SENNA

5. LA SOURCE

6. ANTHONY DAVIDSON

7. AUDI

8. JUAN MANUEL FANGIO

9. WILLIAMS

10. MICHELE ALBORETO

11. MCLAREN

12. PEUGEOT

13. BMW

14. LOTUS

15. RAIDILLON

16. JENSON BUTTON

17. JOHN SURTEES

18. 2012

19. GERHARD BERTER

20. MARTIN BRUNDLE

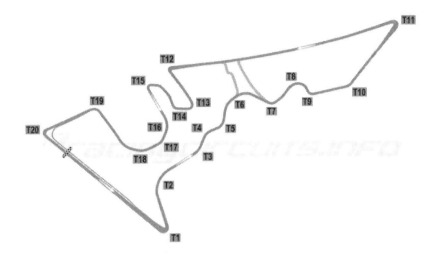

ROUND 3 – ANSWERS

CIRCUIT OF THE AMERICAS

ROUND 3 – CIRCUIT OF THE AMERICAS

1. KEVIN SCHWANTZ

2. LEWIS HAMILTON

3. MARC MARQUEZ

4. ALLAN MCNISH

5. LEWIS HAMILTON

6. JOHAN KRISTOFFERSSON

7. CHIP GANASSI RACING

8. JAMIE WHINCUP

9. ROMAIN GROSJEAN

10. ANDREA IANNONE

11. DANNY KENT

12. TIMO BERNHARD

13. SEBASTIAN VETTEL

14. ALEX RINS

15. CORVETTE

16. FERRARI

17. YAMAHA

18. FERNANDO ALONSO

19. TORO ROSSO

20. DUCATI

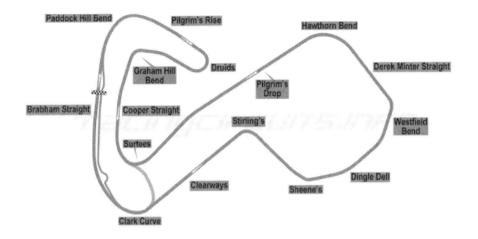

ROUND 4 – ANSWERS

BRANDS HATCH

ROUND 4 – BRANDS HATCH

1. JOHN HOPKINS

2. BRABHAM STRAIGHT

3. NIGEL MANSELL

4. JIM CLARK

5. VAUXHALL

6. JOSH BROOKES

7. ANDY PRIAULX

8. PAUL DI RESTA

9. JAMES TOSELAND

10. NICO HULKENBERG

11. MIKA HAKKINEN

12. KEKE ROSBERG

13. CARLOS REUTEMANN

14. NELSON PIQUET

15. ROB AUSTIN

16. CARL FOGARTY

17. SYLVAIN GUINTOLI

18. JASON PLATO

19. JOCHEN RINDT

20. DRUIDS

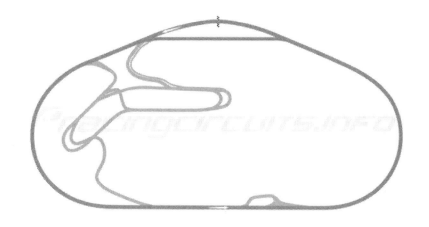

ROUND 5 – ANSWERS

DAYTONA

INTERNATIONAL
SPEEDWAY

ROUND 5 – DAYTONA INTERNATIONAL SPEEDWAY

1. RICHARD PETTY

2. CHEVROLET

3. FLORIDA

4. FERNANDO ALONSO

5. JUSTIN WILSON

6. YAMAHA

7. NICKY HAYDEN

8. KURT BUSCH

9. DALE EARNHARDT JR.

10. PORSCHE

11. DEREK BELL

12. NISSAN

13. CHAZ DAVIES

14. 1971

15. 2012

16. THREE

17. MARIO ANDRETTI

18. FORD

19. JUAN PABLO MONTOYA

20. JAGUAR

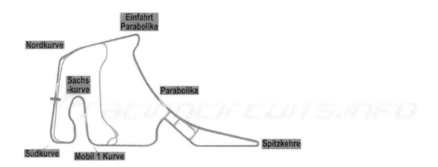

ROUND 6 – ANSWERS

HOCKENHEIMRING

ROUND 6 – HOCKENHEIMRING

1. 1970

2. JOCHEN RINDT

3. MATTIAS EKSTROM

4. PAUL DI RESTA

5. FERNANDO ALONSO

6. AYRTON SENNA

7. NORDKURVE

8. PETTER SOLBERG

9. JOLYON PALMER

10. PHIL READ

11. MICK DOOHAN

12. JIM CLARK

13. NIKI LAUDA

14. VALTTERI BOTTAS

15. FELIPE MASSA

16. LEWIS HAMILTON

17. RENE RAST

18. BMW

19. EDDIE IRVINE

20. RALF SCHUMACHER

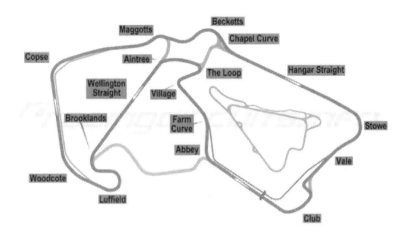

ROUND 7 - ANSWERS

SILVERSTONE

ROUND 7 – SILVERSTONE

1. STOWE

2. GIUSEPPE FARINA

3. JORGE LORENZO

4. JOHAN KRISTOFFERSSON

5. ANDRE LOTTERER

6. GORDON SHEDDEN

7. YAMAHA

8. NIGEL MANSELL

9. DAVID COULTHARD

10. CASEY STONER

11. CAL CRUTCHLOW

12. EMERSON FITTIPALDI

13. MARK WEBBER

14. VALENTINO ROSSI

15. REBELLION RACING

16. TOM CHILTON

17. COPSE

18. JEAN ALESI

19. FREDDIE SPENCER

20. ALAIN PROST

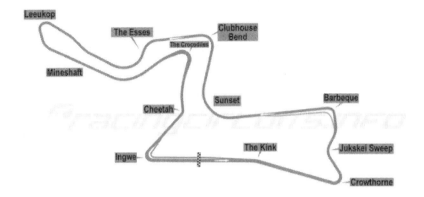

ROUND 8 - ANSWERS

KYALAMI RACING CIRCUIT

ROUND 8 – KYALAMI RACING CIRCUIT

1. 1967

2. ALAIN PROST

3. NORIYUKI HAGA

4. JIM CLARK

5. TYRRELL-FORD

6. DUCATI

7. RONNIE PETERSON

8. COLIN EDWARDS

9. CARL FOGARTY

10. NEEL JANI

11. ANDREA DE CESARIS

12. NIKI LAUDA

13. GILLES VILLENEUVE

14. EUGENE LAVERTY

15. NIGEL MANSELL

16. FERRARI

17. JOCHEN MASS

18. KEKE ROSBERG

19. RENE ARNOUX

20. JACKIE STEWART
☐

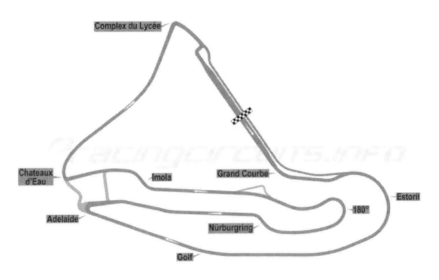

ROUND 9 – ANSWERS

CIRCUIT DE NEVERS

MAGNY-COURS

ROUND 9 – CIRCUIT DE NEVERS MAGNY-COURS

1. HEINZ HARALD-FRENTZEN

2. JORG MULLER

3. WAYNE RAINEY

4. SYLVAIN GUINTOLI

5. NICO ROSBERG

6. MICHAEL SCHUMACHER

7. KIMI RAIKKONEN

8. TOM SYKES

9. CAL CRUTCHLOW

10. TROY BAYLISS

11. FELIPE MASSA

12. RALF SCHUMACHER

13. JAMES TOSELAND

14. JARNO TRULLI

15. MICHAEL SCHUMACHER

16. MCLAREN-MERCEDES

17. MAX BIAGGI

18. RUBENS BARRICHELLO

19. CARLOS CHECA

20. JENSON BUTTON
□

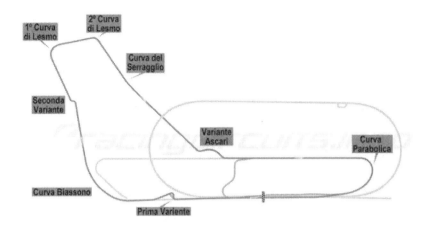

ROUND 10 – ANSWERS

AUTODROMO

NAZIONALE MONZA

ROUND 10 – AUTODROMO NAZIONALE MONZA

1. KENNY ROBERTS

2. JUAN PABLO MONTOYA

3. WAYNE GARDNER

4. RENAULT

5. NIKI LAUDA

6. PHIL HILL

7. TONY BROOKS

8. GERHARD BERGER

9. BARRY SHEENE

10. JOHNNY HERBERT

11. TORO ROSSO

12. EDDIE LAWSON

13. CURVE DI LESMO

14. JOHN SURTEES

15. MASERATI

16. EMERSON FITTIPALDI

17. YVAN MULLER

18. JODY SCHECKTER

19. ANDY PRIAULX

20. RUBENS BARRICHELLO

☐

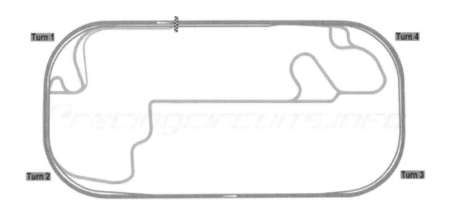

ROUND 11 – ANSWERS

INDIANAPOLIS

MOTOR SPEEDWAY

ROUND 11 – INDIANAPOLIS MOTOR SPEEDWAY

1. THE BRICKYARD

2. JANET GUTHRIE

3. JOHNNIE PARSONS

4. FRENCH

5. WILL POWER

6. JIM CLARK

7. 2012

8. 1994

9. LEWIS HAMILTON

10. JEFF GORDON

11. SEBASTIEN BOURDAIS

12. MARC MARQUEZ

13. FERRARI

14. ALEXANDER ROSSI

15. JUAN PABLO MONTOYA

16. FOUR

17. HONDA

18. KYLE BUSCH

19. CHEVROLET

20. MIKA HAKKINEN

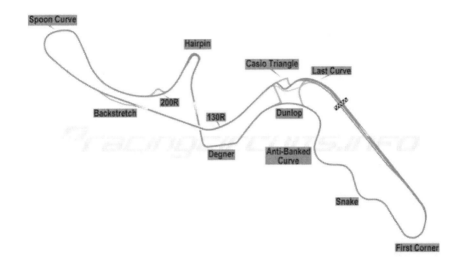

ROUND 12 – ANSWERS

SUZUKA
INTERNATIONAL

RACING COURSE

ROUND 12 – SUZUKA INTERNATIONAL RACING COURSE

1. 1987

2. DAMON HILL

3. VALENTINO ROSSI

4. ALEX LOWES

5. DEGNER CURVE

6. AYRTON SENNA

7. KENNY ROBERTS JR.

8. RICCARDO PATRESE

9. MCLAREN

10. MAX BIAGGI

11. ALESSANDRO NANNINI

12. JOSE MARIA LOPEZ

13. ROBERT HUFF

14. RUBENS BARRICHELLO

15. MCLAREN

16. ZERO

17. YAMAHA

18. HONDA

19. OLIVER TURVEY

20. SEBASTIAN VETTEL

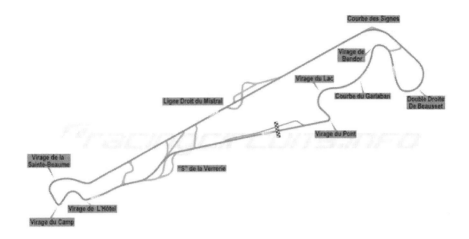

ROUND 13 – ANSWERS

CIRCUIT PAUL RICARD

ROUND 13 – CIRCUIT PAUL RICARD

1. TERRY RYMER

2. ALLAN MCNISH

3. ALAIN PROST

4. 1971

5. YVAN MULLER

6. ALEX CRIVILLE

7. BRENDON HARTLEY

8. SEBASTIEN LOEB

9. RONNIE PETERSON

10. BARRY SHEENE

11. FREDDIE SPENCER

12. RENE ARNOUX

13. KEKE ROSBERG

14. ALAN JONES

15. JAMES HUNT

16. LEWIS HAMILTON

17. JOSE MARIA LOPEZ

18. MICK DOOHAN

19. JACKIE STEWART

20. LOTUS

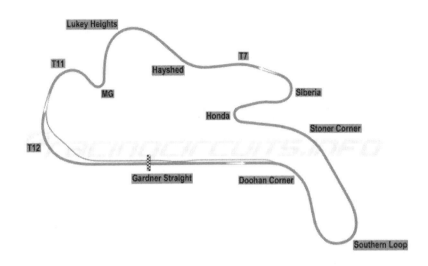

ROUND 14 – ANSWERS

PHILLIP ISLAND

GRAND PRIX CIRCUIT

ROUND 14 – PHILLIP ISLAND GRAND PRIX CIRCUIT

1. 1990

2. 1935

3. FABIAN COULTHARD

4. CASEY STONER

5. HONDA

6. HOLDEN

7. GARDNER STRAIGHT

8. CARL FOGARTY

9. SHANE VAN GISBERGEN

10. SPAIN

11. CAL CRUTCHLOW

12. TROY CORSER

13. HONDA

14. LEON HASLAM

15. TWO

16. WAYNE GARDNER

17. TROY BAYLISS

18. TOM SYKES

19. JORGE LORENZO

20. BRAD BINDER

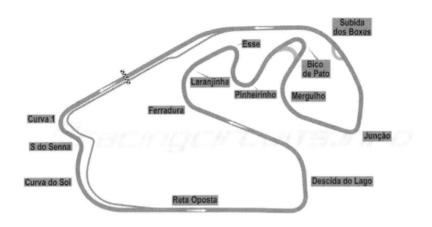

ROUND 15 – ANSWERS

AUTODROMO

JOSE CARLOS PACE

P a g e | **148**

ROUND 15 – AUTODROMO JOSE CARLOS PACE

1. INTERLAGOS

2. ALEXANDER WURZ

3. RICARDO ZONTA

4. CARLOS REUTEMANN

5. NIGEL MANSELL

6. ROMAIN DUMAS

7. ALAIN PROST

8. EMERSON FITTIPALDI

9. NICO ROSBERG

10. JACQUES VILLENEUVE

11. JENSON BUTTON

12. FELIPE MASSA

13. JUAN PABLO MONTOYA

14. FOUR

15. GIANCARLO FISICHELLA

16. JACQUES LAFFITE

17. NIKI LAUDA

18. ANDRE LOTTERER

19. AYRTON SENNA

20. MIKA HAKKINEN

ROUND 16 – ANSWERS

SNAEFELL

MOUNTAIN COURSE

ROUND 16 – SNAEFELL MOUNTAIN COURSE

1. GIACOMO AGOSTINI

2. 1985

3. CARL FOGARTY

4. 1976

5. NORTON

6. BRUCE ANSTEY

7. PHIL READ

8. GRAEME CROSBY

9. JOEY DUNLOP

10. YAMAHA

11. 2010

12. JOHN MCGUINNESS

13. STEVE HISLOP

14. 1911

15. IAN HUTCHINSON

16. GEOFF DUKE

17. JIM REDMAN

18. FOUR

19. MICHAEL DUNLOP

20. SUZUKI

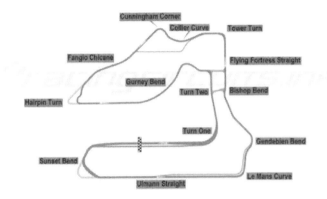

ROUND 17 – ANSWERS

SEBRING

INTERNATIONAL RACEWAY

ROUND 17 – SEBRING INTERNATIONAL RACEWAY

1. BRUCE MCLAREN

2. KAZUKI NAKAJIMA

3. WILL STEVENS

4. PORSCHE

5. FELIPE NASR

6. TONY BROOKS

7. GIANMARIA BRUNI

8. ALLAN MCNISH

9. JACKY ICKX

10. JACK BRABHAM

11. MIKE CONWAY

12. HONDA

13. OLIVIER PANIS

14. ALEX LYNN

15. WOLFGANG VON TRIPS

16. MASERATI

17. DEREK DALY

18. BRENDON HARTLEY

19. SIX

20. JOHNNY HERBERT

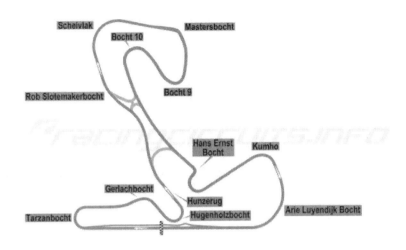

ROUND 18 – ANSWERS

CIRCUIT ZANDVOORT

ROUND 18 – CIRCUIT ZANDVOORT

1. TIMO SCHEIDER

2. DAVID COULTHARD

3. JIM CLARK

4. NIKI LAUDA

5. GARY PAFFETT

6. ALBERTO ASCARI

7. PAUL DI RESTA

8. TYRRELL

9. FRANCE

10. NELSON PIQUET

11. FERRARI

12. THREE

13. LOUIS ROSIER

14. ALAN JONES

15. TIMO GLOCK

16. MATTIAS EKSTROM

17. 1993

18. VALTTERI BOTTAS

19. 2005

20. FERRARI

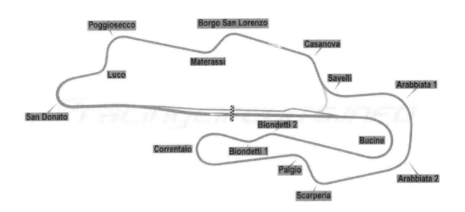

ROUND 19 – ANSWERS

MUGELLO CIRCUIT

ROUND 19 – MUGELLO CIRCUIT

1. 1976

2. DOUG POLEN

3. JAMIE GREEN

4. ANDREA DOVIZIOSO

5. JORGE LORENZO

6. RAYMOND ROCHE

7. CASEY STONER

8. VALENTINO ROSSI

9. A1GP

10. YAMAHA

11. KEVIN SCHWANTZ

12. 1991

13. BRADLEY SMITH

14. ANDREA DOVIZIOSO

15. ALEX BARROS

16. KENNY ROBERTS

17. MAX BIAGGI

18. MARCO SIMONCELLI

19. SCOTT REDDING

20. JORGE LORENZO

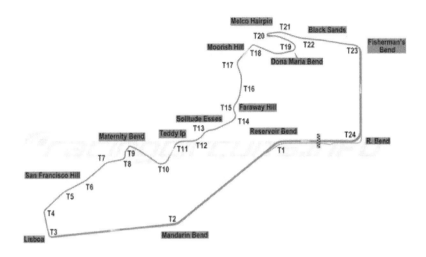

ROUND 20 – ANSWERS

GUIA CIRCUIT

ROUND 20 – GUIA CIRCUIT

1. RESERVOIR

2. STUART EASTON

3. BMW

4. SWITZERLAND

5. ROBERT HUFF

6. RALF SCHUMACHER

7. ANTONIO FELIX DA COSTA

8. MIKE CONWAY

9. CARL FOGARTY

10. MICHAEL RUTTER

11. TIM HARVEY

12. MARO ENGEL

13. YAMAHA

14. FELIX ROSENQVIST

15. DAN TICKTUM

16. ALEX LYNN

17. CITROEN

18. THREE

19. JOHN MCGUINNESS

20. 1983

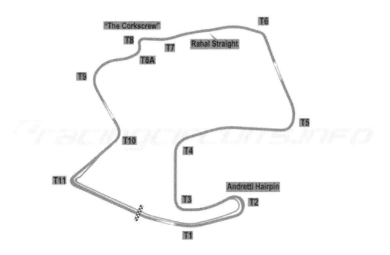

ROUND 21 – ANSWERS

LAGUNA SECA RACEWAY

ROUND 21 – LAGUNA SECA RACEWAY

1. THE CORKSCREW

2. MARC MARQUEZ

3. ALEX ZANARDI

4. TOM SYKES

5. DANI PEDROSA

6. PIPO DERANI

7. JONATHAN REA

8. CHRIS VERMEULEN

9. JACQUES VILLENEUVE

10. PATRICK CARPENTIER

11. NICKY HAYDEN

12. MARKUS WINKELHOCK

13. CHAZ DAVIES

14. HELIO CASTRONEVES

15. MARIO ANDRETTI

16. STIRLING MOSS

17. TWO

18. COLIN EDWARDS

19. BOBBY RAHAL

20. EDDIE LAWSON

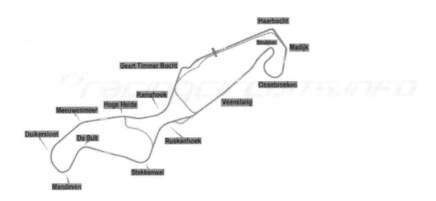

ROUND 22 – ANSWERS

TT CIRCUIT ASSEN

ROUND 22 – TT CIRCUIT ASSEN

1. SHANE BYRNE

2. JACK MILLER

3. MAVERICK VINALES

4. MIKE HAILWOOD

5. TOM SYKES

6. HONDA

7. DANILO PETRUCCI

8. CHRISTIAN IDDON

9. CASEY STONER

10. JOSH BROOKES

11. JONATHAN REA

12. ANDREA DOVIZIOSO

13. JUSTIN WILSON

14. ALEX LOWES

15. LEON HASLAM

16. JOHANN ZARCO

17. BEN SPIES

18. SUZUKI

19. BARRY SHEENE

20. GIACOMO AGOSTINI

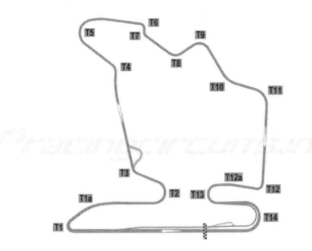

ROUND 23 – ANSWERS

HUNGARORING

ROUND 23 - HUNGARORING

1. NELSON PIQUET

2. YVAN MULLER

3. MICK DOOHAN

4. EDDIE LAWSON

5. TIAGO MONTEIRO

6. BMW

7. HONDA

8. LEWIS HAMILTON

9. MCLAREN

10. DANIEL RICCIARDO

11. HONDA

12. NIGEL MANSELL

13. THIERRY BOUTSEN

14. ALAIN PROST

15. MARTIN BRUNDLE

16. MICHAEL SCHUMACHER

17. EDDIE IRVINE

18. TWO

19. 1996

20. HEIKKI KOVALAINEN

ROUND 24 – ANSWERS

NURBURGRING

ROUND 24 – NURBURGRING

1. JACKIE STEWART

2. ALAIN PROST

3. FERNANDO ALONSO

4. MICK DOOHAN

5. 1970

6. NIKI LAUDA

7. JACQUES VILLENEUVE

8. MICHELE ALBORETO

9. JOHNNY HERBERT

10. LEWIS HAMILTON

11. CLAY REGAZZONI

12. ALBERTO ASCARI

13. JAMES HUNT

14. MERCEDES

15. MIKA HAKKINEN

16. RALF SCHUMACHER

17. FERRARI

18. JACKY ICKX

19. GRAHAM HILL

20. RUBENS BARRICHELLO

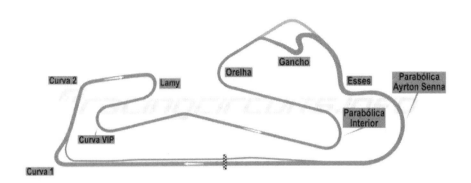

ROUND 25 – ANSWERS

AUTODROMO DO ESTORIL

ROUND 25 – AUTODROMO DO ESTORIL

1. NELSON PIQUET JR.

2. HARRY TINCKNELL

3. GABRIELE TARQUINI

4. JORGE LORENZO

5. AYRTON SENNA

6. ALAIN PROST

7. JAMES NASH

8. BENETTON

9. STEFAN BRADL

10. CHEVROLET

11. WILLIAMS

12. RICCARDO PATRESE

13. YAMAHA

14. CASEY STONER

15. DAMON HILL

16. GERHARD BERGER

17. DANI PEDROSA

18. HYUNDAI

19. HEINZ-HARALD FRENTZEN

20. FERRARI

ROUND 26 – ANSWERS

CIRCUIT GILLES VILLENEUVE

ROUND 26 – CIRCUIT GILLES VILLENEUVE

1. DARIO FRANCHITTI

2. MARK BLUNDELL

3. NELSON PIQUET

4. PATRICK TAMBAY

5. MICHAEL SCHUMACHER

6. CASINO STRAIGHT or DROIT DU CASINO

7. ROBERT KUBICA

8. RALF SCHUMACHER

9. STEFAN JOHANSSON

10. JONATHAN PALMER

11. JJ LEHTO

12. JEAN ALESI

13. EDDIE IRVINE

14. KIMI RAIKKONEN

15. DAMON HILL

16. JORDAN

17. LANCE STROLL

18. JENSON BUTTON

19. ALEXANDER WURZ

20. MICHAEL SCHUMACHER

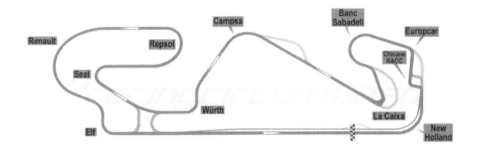

ROUND 27 – ANSWERS

CIRCUIT DE

BARCELONA-CATALUNYA

ROUND 27 – CIRCUIT DE BARCELONA-CATALUNYA

1. PETTER SOLBERG

2. 1996

3. NIGEL MANSELL

4. MATTIAS EKSTROM

5. MICK DOOHAN

6. ZERO

7. JOHAN KRISTOFFERSSON

8. MARK BLUNDELL

9. ANDREA DOVIZIOSO

10. TIMMY HANSEN

11. TOOMAS HEIKKINEN

12. ANDREAS BAKKERUD

13. DUCATI

14. DANNY KENT

15. VALENTINO ROSSI

16. MIKA HAKKINEN

17. MAX VERSTAPPEN

18. PASTOR MALDONADO

19. FELIPE MASSA

20. ONE

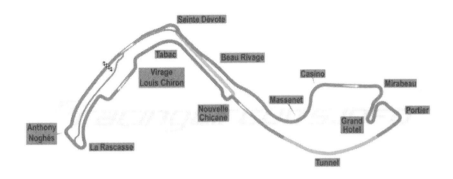

ROUND 28 – ANSWERS

CIRCUIT DE MONACO

ROUND 28 – CIRCUIT DE MONACO

1. JUAN MANUEL FANGIO

2. SEBASTIEN BUEMI

3. NICO ROSBERG

4. AYRTON SENNA

5. ROMAIN GROSJEAN

6. JEAN-ERIC VERGNE

7. NYCK DE VRIES

8. DANIEL RICCIARDO

9. MCLAREN

10. THREE

11. GRAHAM HILL

12. OLIVIER PANIS

13. LOTUS

14. STIRLING MOSS

15. SERGIO PEREZ

16. NICK HEIDFELD

17. DENNY HULME

18. 1981

19. RUBENS BARRICHELLO

20. MARK WEBBER

ROUND 29 – ANSWERS

DONINGTON PARK

ROUND 29 – DONINGTON PARK

1. YVAN MULLER

2. MAURO BALDI

3. TOM SYKES

4. MARCO MELANDRI

5. NARAIN KARTHIKEYAN

6. JOHNNY HERBERT

7. ALAIN PROST

8. RYUICHI KIYONARI

9. GORDON SHEDDEN

10. ZAK BROWN

11. LEON HASLAM

12. COLIN TURKINGTON

13. SHANE BYRNE

14. CASEY STONER

15. COLIN EDWARDS

16. CHRISTIAN FITTIPALDI

17. TOM ONSLOW-COLE

18. JOSH BROOKES

19. KENNY ROBERTS JR.

20. MICHAEL ANDRETTI

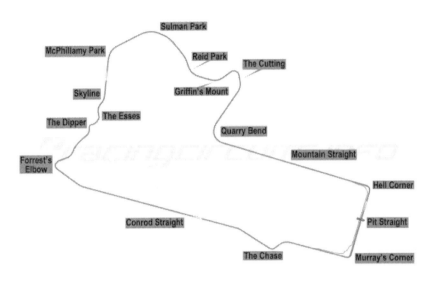

ROUND 30 – ANSWERS

MOUNT PANORAMA

ROUND 30 – MOUNT PANORAMA

1. HELL CORNER

2. MICK DOOHAN

3. RICKARD RYDELL

4. HOLDEN

5. THE DIPPER

6. MAZDA

7. MCLAREN

8. MIKA SALO

9. DAVID BRABHAM

10. 1991

11. 1960

12. ALLAN SIMONSEN

13. NISSAN

14. PORSCHE

15. MURRAYS CORNER

16. PETER BROCK

17. CRAIG LOWNDES

18. JAMIE WHINCUP

19. DARRYL O'YOUNG

20. TOYOTA

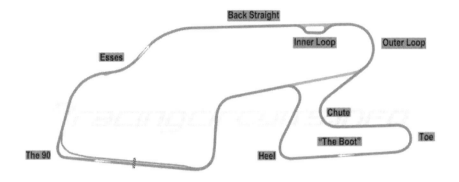

ROUND 31 – ANSWERS

WATKINS GLEN

ROUND 31 – WATKINS GLEN

1. TONY STEWART

2. CADILLAC

3. RYAN HUNTER-REAY

4. INNES IRELAND

5. CHEVROLET

6. MARIO ANDRETTI

7. SCOTT DIXON

8. FRANCOIS CEVERT

9. JUAN PABLO MONTOYA

10. DEREK BELL

11. HONDA

12. JAMES HUNT

13. GILLES VILLENEUVE

14. DENNY HAMLIN

15. RONNIE PETERSON

16. JOCHEN RINDT

17. ROLF STOMMELEN

18. CARLOS REUTEMANN

19. BRM

20. HESKETH

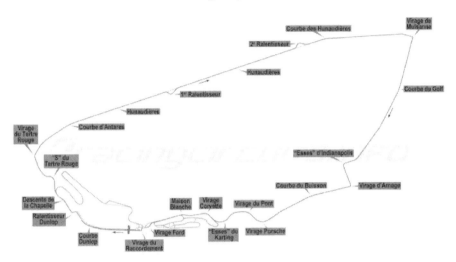

ROUND 32 – ANSWERS

CIRCUIT DE LA SARTHE

THE 24 QUESTIONS

OF

LE MANS

ROUND 32 – CIRCUIT DE LA SARTHE

1. DEREK BELL

2. PORSCHE

3. TOM KRISTENSEN

4. ARNAGE

5. NICK TANDY

6. TIMO BERNHARD

7. PORSCHE

8. NEEL JANI

9. FRANCE

10. SIX

11. ALFA ROMEO

12. BRUCE MCLAREN

13. MICHELE ALBORETO

14. JOHNNY HERBERT

15. GRAHAM HILL

16. DAVY JONES

17. 1983

18. PEUGEOT

19. BENTLEY

20. NICO HULKENBERG

21. TETRE ROUGE

22. 1936

23. MIKE HAWTHORN

24. PHIL HILL

CHAMPIONSHIP POINTS

STANDINGS

To assist your Quiz Prix Championship with friends, on the following pages are boxes with space for 7 players against each of the circuits you compete at.

Allocate a player number and fill in the boxes of the relevant circuits with your championship points and total them up at the end.

It may be advisable to use a pencil so these points can be erased and used again.

If there are more than 8 eight players please use the extra boxes provided.

CIRCUIT	1	2	3	4	5	6	7
AUTODROMO JUAN Y OSCAR GALVEZ							
CIRCUIT DE SPA-FRANCORCHAMPS							
CIRCUIT OF THE AMERICAS							
BRANDS HATCH							
DAYTONA INTERNATIONAL SPEEDWAY							
HOCKENHEIMRING							
SILVERSTONE							
KYALAMI RACING CIRCUIT							
CIRCUIT DE NEVERS MAGNY-COURS							
AUTODROMO NAZIONALE MONZA							
INDIANAPOLIS MOTOR SPEEDWAY							
SUZUKA INTERNATIONAL RACING COURSE							
CIRCUIT PAUL RICARD							
PHILLIP ISLAND GRAND PRIX CIRCUIT							
AUTODROMO JOSE CARLOS PACE							
SNAEFELL MOUNTAIN COURSE							

SEBRING INTERNATIONAL RACEWAY							
CIRCUIT ZANDVOORT							
MUGELLO CIRCUIT							
GUIA CIRCUIT							
LAGUNA SECA RACEWAY							
TT CIRCUIT ASSEN							
HUNGARORING							
NURBURGRING							
AUTODROMO DO ESTORIL							
CIRCUIT GILLES VILLENEUVE							
CIRCUIT DE BARCELONA-CATALUNYA							
CIRCUIT DE MONACO							
DONINGTON PARK							
MOUNT PANORAMA							
WATKINS GLEN							
CIRCUIT DE LA SARTHE							
TOTAL POINTS							

CIRCUIT							
AUTODROMO JUAN Y OSCAR GALVEZ							
CIRCUIT DE SPA-FRANCORCHAMPS							
CIRCUIT OF THE AMERICAS							
BRANDS HATCH							
DAYTONA INTERNATIONAL SPEEDWAY							
HOCKENHEIMRING							
SILVERSTONE							
KYALAMI RACING CIRCUIT							
CIRCUIT DE NEVERS MAGNY-COURS							
AUTODROMO NAZIONALE MONZA							
INDIANAPOLIS MOTOR SPEEDWAY							
SUZUKA INTERNATIONAL RACING COURSE							
CIRCUIT PAUL RICARD							
PHILLIP ISLAND GRAND PRIX CIRCUIT							
AUTODROMO JOSE CARLOS PACE							
SNAEFELL MOUNTAIN COURSE							

SEBRING INTERNATIONAL RACEWAY							
CIRCUIT ZANDVOORT							
MUGELLO CIRCUIT							
GUIA CIRCUIT							
LAGUNA SECA RACEWAY							
TT CIRCUIT ASSEN							
HUNGARORING							
NURBURGRING							
AUTODROMO DO ESTORIL							
CIRCUIT GILLES VILLENEUVE							
CIRCUIT DE BARCELONA-CATALUNYA							
CIRCUIT DE MONACO							
DONINGTON PARK							
MOUNT PANORAMA							
WATKINS GLEN							
CIRCUIT DE LA SARTHE							

TOTAL POINTS							

Printed in Great Britain
by Amazon

46602514R00113